Basque Classics Series
No. 12

Series Editors

William A. Douglass
Gregorio Monreal
Pello Salaburu

Downhill

and

Rock & Core

Gabriel Aresti

Translated by Amaia Gabantxo

With an introduction by Jon Kortazar

and a preface by Joseba Zulaika

Center for Basque Studies
University of Nevada, Reno

This book was published with generous financial support obtained by the Association of Friends of the Center for Basque Studies and from the Provincial Government of Bizkaia.

Basque Classics Series, no. 12
Series Editors: William A. Douglass, Gregorio Monreal, and Pello Salaburu

William A. Douglass Center for Basque Studies
University of Nevada, Reno
Reno, Nevada 89557
http://basque.unr.edu

Translation by Amaia Gabantxo

Published with permission of the Gabriel Aresti Foundation
Originally published: *Maldan behera* (*Revista Euskera de la Academia de la Lengua Vasca*, 1959) and *Harri eta herri* (Zarautz: Itxaropena, 1964).

Library of Congress Cataloging-in-Publication Data

Names: Aresti, Gabriel, author. | Gabantxo, Amaia, translator. | Kortazar, Jon, writer of introduction. | Zulaika, Joseba, writer of foreword.
Title: Downhill and Rock and Core / Gabriel Aresti ; translated by Amaia Gabantxo, with an introduction by Jon Kortazar and foreword by Joseba Zulaika.
Description: Reno, NV : Center for Basque Studies, [2017] | Series: Basque classics series ; No. 12 | Includes bibliographical references and index.
Identifiers: LCCN 2017006426 (print) | LCCN 2017006884 (ebook) | ISBN 9781935709756 (hardcover : alk. paper) | ISBN 9781935709763 (pbk. : alk. paper) | ISBN 9781935709770
Classification: LCC PH5339.A7 A2 2017 (print) | LCC PH5339.A7 (ebook) | DDC 899/.921--dc23
LC record available at https://lccn.loc.gov/2017006426

Contents

Foreword

ARESTI: A RED DAWN IS BREAKING

Gabriel Aresti was the essential poet for my Basque generation of the 1960s. "If you want to write me/You know where I am," he wrote, "In this most slippery hell/In the mouth of the devil." It was the hell of Franco's repressive regime, the endless darkness of his city, Bilbao, turned into an industrial and cultural wasteland. Aresti was the crucified Bilbao writer howling for justice and truth, the vulnerable man of eternal downfall who created a new poetics and a new subjectivity.

Aresti chose *oskorria* (red sky, twilight, dawn) as the emblematic image of the Basque Country he dreamed and willed—her destiny both crepuscular and revolutionary. Aresti's trepidant anthem, sung by the Bilbao folk group Oskorri, brought us to our feet: "We heard a war cry/marching before a sword./A red dawn is breaking/in the land of the Basques." It was the dusk of Franco's nightmare and ETA's inaugural martyrdom, the crisis of Christianity tempered by new *red* beliefs among Bilbao's proletarian working classes. The red skies formed by the glare of molten metal in the blast furnaces of Nevion's Left Bank would soon disappear as the fabled Altos Hornos ironworks closed down and were replaced by the new Guggenheim-era gentrified urbanizations.

In 1959, the year ETA was born, he wrote his first major work, *Maldan behera (Downhill),* a long initiation poem of descent into hell and final ascension—a prophecy for my generation. It begins: "Because my spirit today/wants to flee the mountain/Downhill fast/my naked body goes." Christian and atheist at once, epigraphs from Nietzsche and Christ preceded it. The poet's Dantesque voyage celebrates the twilight of the Gods and calls for the city's revival. The poem's second part opens with an antithetical quatrain: "My winged soul/ flies happy heavenward,/my body lies and rots/down on the earth below." The image evokes the lines written by the poet Lauaxeta, arrested in Gernika after its bombing, the morning he faced the firing squad in July of 1937: "Let my soul go to luminous heaven/my body to the dark earth below." If the poet is to uphold the torch of an Ideal City, he must be ready to fight for justice, suffer persecution, die. In its final section, *Maldan gora* (Ascent), the poem closes the classic initiation cycle of descent, death, and resurrection.

By parodying a prophet who descends from the mountaintop to preach his gospel, Aresti subjected himself to the vital antagonisms of his city: Basque and Castilian, Gernika and the working class, natives and immigrants, nationalism and socialism, Christ and Zarathustra. He had to be split asunder himself in order to conceive a new identity and life for his city—the Bilbao of urban and ecological devastation, its Basque culture and language dying, a museum of horrors that he compared to Dante's suffering city.

"If you ever think of me," Aresti told his future biographer in their first casual encounter, "remember that you have known a wretched man who suffers much." He was the luminous writer who had recreated the native Euskara (he learned it as an adult) on the basis of its poetic improvisational verse-singing tradition and informed by contemporary literature. His *Harri eta Herri* (*Rock & Core*) became the inaugural text for a new Basque literature grounded on the premise that language is the foundation of culture and knowledge. He taught my generation that aesthetics alone is not enough, that there is always the question of justice. I met him while I was a student at the University of Deusto in Bilbao. When he was hospitalized I visited him; he was delighted that I was going abroad to study anthropology. Days later I was one of the young writers carrying his casket at the cemetery in Derio. He had died singing his prophetic song *Oskorria*—"a red dawn is breaking in the land of the Basques." We distributed his best-known poem, translated into dozens of languages, "I will defend my father's house." Like many of my generation I had become a writer under his influence; his death became a mandate to write. He was forty-one.

—*Joseba Zulaika*

TRANSLATOR'S PREFACE

I felt an enormous responsibility when I was asked to translate Gabriel Aresti's *Maldan behera* and *Harri eta herri*. Not only because of what these two works symbolize in Basque literature—radical new chapters in its history, among its most important steps toward modernity—but because some of the poems in these two collections had been with me since childhood and I didn't know if I'd be able to envision them in any other form but the original Basque in which they first inhabited my consciousness. Gabriel Aresti was the first Basque poet that I was fully conscious of. I still remember the black-and-white, Chillida-designed cover of the copy of *Harri eta herri* we had at home, reading it and finding a poetry so immediate and close to the life outside our front door that it shocked me with its intimacy. I must have been thirteen or fourteen at the time. I had read other Basque poets in my evening Basque classes, sang many Basque songs composed by Basque poets before, but this was different. A whole new world of possibility. I suddenly understood: it's not just pretty words, this is what poetry can do.

> *They'll say*
> *this*
> *ain't poetry*
> *and*
> *I'll tell them*
> *poetry*
> *is*
> *a hammer.*

That little poem, in many ways, shaped my thought. I took a whole day to write it in beautiful block letters on the cover of one of my school folders. It made me understand the power of the word to destroy, to alter, to undo—and to construct, to rebuild. And the graft of the poetic endeavor. And the essential human need for it. These days, it's one of the first poems I introduce my students and my audiences to, and it never fails to astound, to move, to stir something within.

Aresti wrote these two collections in the midst of hard times for the Basque Country. Franco's regime opposed all manifestations of Basque culture, (unsuccessfully) trying to erase it. Writing in Basque at the time was nothing short of an activist pursuit—learning Basque too, which Aresti did only as an adult. Despite the intrinsic riches of Euskara (age does make things, if not better, at least always more interesting and complex), we didn't have a proper written literary tradition in Basque, but a sparse collection of writings that couldn't be said to amount to a cohesive whole. And at the heart of this thinly threaded cloth was a void: the Basque language never had a great epic poem like *Beowulf* or *El Cantar del Mio Cid* or *La Chanson de Roland* and, without that, how could we claim a literary tradition? Moreover, how could we build a canon if our language lacked the main essential block upon which literary canons are built?

One thing Basques intimately understand is the void. The presence of absence. Our philosophers, artists, and poets have written about it at large (see Jorge Oteiza for a start). Our pre-Christian goddess Mayi (Mari, Amari) fed off the void, off everything that isn't, and maybe it is because of her that our souls are particularly well acquainted and at ease with absence—our country is not a country; our language is a mystery. It's all right, she teaches, some things are visible (or tangible) and others invisible (or intangible), and there are more of the later—so let's drink from there. There's abundance there.

Literary translators are a bit like actors, we take on the spirit of our authors. So what if we don't have an epic poem, I imagined Aresti thinking in a typically pragmatic Basque way: *How do I build a tradition out of no-tradition?* We have *bertsolaritza*, a popular improvised verse singing tradition that's as old as the mountains and as rich as any epic poem. So what if we have only a few, mostly ecclesiastical writings—let's bring them into the mix. What if our epic hero, given the innate Basque disdain for heralded nobility, was a man of the street. *Maybe*, I imagined him thinking, *I can cook up something like a modern epic poem out of all this*. And he wrote *Maldan behera*—*Downhill* in my translation—bringing together the legacies of Basque literature he had and didn't have at the time: *bertsolaritza* (oral) and ecclesiastical (written), and weaving them into a Nietzschean sort of epic poem, because modernism and modern philosophy hadn't properly manifested in poetic form in Basque. So he added that, Marxist that he was. He created a nihilistic antihero to upend the religiosity that impregnated Basque literary language, and for form, used the incisive and —sometimes dark—humor and rhythmic playfulness of *bertsolaritza* to add musicality and movement and lightness to the whole, and to link his work to the poetics of the people (versus the poetics of religion).

A few years later, still thinking about the poetics of the people and seeking to find a form alternate to *bertsolaritza*, he wrote *Harri eta herri—Rock & Core* in my translation. In it, he, Gabriel Aresti, was the antihero; the antipoet. *They'll say/this/ain't poetry*. It's a defiant collection that finds poetry in the voice and the actions of the common, working man. The poet is also a common, tough, working man: words are his hammer and nails. Common Basque became literary Basque. Stripped, streetwise, straight-talking, spunky. This poetry *was* a hammer, and it broke and rebuilt Basque literary language for the generations of writers that came after Aresti.

Writing *Downhill* and *Rock & Core* in English has been an enticing, fascinating, and sometimes agonizing challenge. Aresti's poetry in English will never do what it did in Basque; the process of carrying these two collections over to the English language in 2017 transforms them into completely different beasts to the beasts they were in 1959 and 1964 in their literary and existential contexts. But I hope that readers of these two collections will be able catch a glimpse of their power and beauty, and enjoy my attempt at channeling the soul and poetic imagination of the man who did so much for Basque literature and the portrayal of the indomitable Basque spirit.

Walter Benjamin wrote about translation as the extended life of a literary work of art. As I close and file away the folders of a project that has taken up most of a year of my life and remember the child that I was carefully etching Aresti's poem into a school notebook in a strange echo of the future, I'd like to say here that I am profoundly honored to have had the opportunity to contribute to Gabriel Aresti's literary afterlife.

—Amaia Gabantxo
Chicago, January 2017

Introduction

GABRIEL ARESTI, FROM SYMBOLISM TO SOCIAL CONSCIOUSNESS

Jon Kortazar

Gabriel Aresti (1933–1975) was a prominent figure in the panorama of Basque-language literature from the early 1960s until his death in 1975. His presence in the cultural and social panorama, in the context of Basque literature and culture of the time, a period convulsed by profound social and political change, was constant and enriching.

The writer Gabriel Aresti was born in Bilbao to a lower-middle-class family with some connections to the political circles of the day. His father was a city councilor in Bilbao and a known activist in the Falange, one of the extreme-right-wing parties that supported General Franco's (1892-1975) regime. Starting in 1948, Aresti pursued a business degree, which would ensure his professional survival as an accountant for various firms in Bilbao and its metropolitan area. At that time, at the Bilbao Business School (*Escuela de Comercio*), he began to learn Basque on his own and to recover it as part of his heritage, since his father's family came from a Basque-speaking area of Bizkaia. Following a failed engagement to a woman from a well-known Basque nationalist family in Bilbao, which led to a severe ideological and personal crisis for Aresti, he married Meli Esteban, the daughter of Spanish immigrants from the province of León, in 1960. In order to understand this fact, which Aresti himself described as a central turning point in his thinking, it is necessary to keep in mind the deep gulf that the nationalist ideology as-

* This introduction is part of the LAIDA (Literatura eta identitatea) Research Project, a member of the network of research groups financed by the Basque Government (IT 1012/16).

sociated with the Basque Nationalist Party (Basque: Euzko Alderdi Jeltzalea, EAJ; Spanish: Partido Nacionalista Vasco; acronym EAJ-PNV)[1] at the time established between Basques and non-Basques, who were the object of a certain degree of xenophobia and whose acceptance in society was limited. In the society of the day, marrying a non-Basque woman meant censure, criticism, upheaval, and a change in social class, and it brought ostracism with it. The couple had three daughters, Nerea, Guria, and Andere Bihotz, and lost a fourth a few days after birth.

Aresti worked as an accountant in a variety of industries, a career that he combined with writing and cultural activity. Starting in 1972, his rhythm of work began to decrease as a consequence of liver disease, not cirrhosis, as is often said, but a collapse produced by deficient metabolism of lead. He died in June 1975 following an operation aimed at alleviating his illness, a few months before the death of the dictator Franco.

Cultural Activity

Gabriel Aresti's presence in the Basque Country's cultural panorama should be the object of careful attention, since his importance stems equally from his literary works and from the cultural initiatives that he carried out in the course of his intellectual career.

His great task was the modernization of Basque culture, which was still governed by the ideological, political, and aesthetic conditions created under the Spanish Republic, before the Spanish Civil War (1936–39), and designed and led by the Basque Nationalist Party with its confessional and Christian Democratic character. By 1960, these conditions were at least open to question and poorly adapted to the social crisis that was already perceptible and would explode in 1968. The persistence of Franco's dictatorship was of little help when it came to the evolution of nationalist intellectual society's ideological and cultural presuppositions; rather, it contributed to their sclerosis, so that the ideological hallmarks defined in the 1930s remained in place in the

1. The Basque Nationalist Party was founded by Sabino Arana at the end of the nineteenth century (1895) with the aim of promoting national consciousness in the Basque Country. It initially called for independence from Spain but later tilted in favor of autonomy. It encouraged Basque culture, but its more conservative inclinations led it to maintain a purist attitude toward the essence of Basqueness, which it defined as "God and *fueros* (traditional laws and privileges)," with a markedly negative attitude toward immigration from other regions of Spain. It subsequently evolved in the direction of Christian Democracy and today is moving toward non-confessional humanism. It has been the majority party in Basque society since the reestablishment of autonomy in 1979. See www.eaj-pnv.eus.

1960s, accentuating their hegemonic character in nationalist society: clericalism, the decisive importance of religion in society, political conservatism, criticism of socialism, anticommunism, and a certain degree of passivity with regard to Franco's regime. This conservative nationalist ideological system also included elements related to aesthetics and to the conception of the Basque language and Basque-language literature, which we will mention later.

The writer Gabriel Aresti designed and carried out a cultural project that would develop a system that brought this cultural environment originating in previous decades into crisis. First of all, he called for a lay culture that would marginalize clerical leadership of Basque culture, predominant at the time. It was in this spirit that he published his books and promoted the creation of the Kriselu (1968–69) and Lur (1970) publishing houses, channels for the subsequent promotion of Basque literature. He very soon (1959) came into contact with Bilbao's socialist and communist circles at the La Concordia café, where he met Bilbao poets and writers with Marxist leanings who gradually introduced him to social issues and a critique of Bilbao's economic situation under Franco. He also conducted a critique of the Church's positions. These bitter debates began in 1968. Basque conservatives maligned him as a Hispanophile (*españolista*) and a Marxist, two criticisms against which it was difficult to defend under a dictatorship: it was impossible to say that one was not a Spaniard without attracting the intervention of the police.

In addition, Aresti renewed awareness of the Basque language in his time, proposing the unification of Basque beginning in 1963. As is well known, a group of philologists and linguists approved the basis for linguistic unification in 1968, at a conference held at the convent of Arantzazu,[2] in a region and at a site emblematic of Basque culture due to the fact that the renovation of the local church became a very important focus for the creation of Basque art. Nevertheless, the conservative hegemonic culture of the day followed the linguistic principles that the

2. Readers interested in the topic of linguistic unification should consult Pello Salaburu, *Writing Words: The Unique Case of the Standardization of Basque* (Reno: Center for Basque Studies, University of Nevada, Reno, 2015), Pello Salaburu and Xabier Alberdi, "The Search for a Common Code," included in the volume *The Challenge of a Bilingual Society in the Basque Country*, ed. Pello Salaburu and Xabier Alberdi, Current Reseaerch Series (Center for Basque Studies, University of Nevada, Reno, 2012), 93–113, and *Koldo Mitxelena: Selected Writings of a Basque Scholar*, compiled and with an introduction by Pello Salaburu, Basque Classics Series (Center for Basque Studies, University of Nevada, Reno, 2008).

PNV's founder, Sabino Arana, had imposed. Put briefly, the aim was a purism that would root out any trace of Romance influence on Basque, whether from Latin or from Spanish. The first consequence was the creation of neologisms that gradually replaced the words habitually used by Basque speakers in daily life. The second was the opening up of an unbridgeable gap between written and spoken usage. The third consequence, however, was perhaps the most extreme: every author considered himself authorized to put forward his own vocabulary and his own morphology, no longer in place of the spoken language, but rather of previous purist proposals that the author judged insufficiently pure. In this way, the written language was taken to such an extreme that an author could put forward a linguistic register that had only a single person who cultivated or understood it: the author himself. An example illustrating the unhelpfulness of the suffocating situation under Franco was the publication, right at the end of 1959, of a translation of the Gospels and the Acts of the Apostles by the extreme purist Manuel Arriandiaga (1879–1947) (Laka 1987), a translation so full of words invented by the author that it was not merely removed from normal speech, but simply unintelligible. The word "*Goizparraik*" to refer to the Gospels was derived, according to the author's personal interpretation, from a compound of *goi+hitz+barri*, "the good news [that comes] from above," with an article ending in "*-ik*," and not in "*-ak*" as is usual in Basque.

Aresti found the title given to the translation, *Goizparraik eta Beldubaik Egiñak*, ironic and offered it as an example of what should not be done in literature. In effect, he harshly criticized the language used in the volume: "And so evolution continues until it reaches Arriandiaga and the other purists, who are purity-mongers [*puristazos*]. Purity-mongers who have arrived at the most tremendous absurdities. In linguistic matters in Basque, every imaginable record has been broken" (Aresti 1986c, 81).

For this reason, he proposed a literary style that was close to everyday speech. This position conflicted with the other tendency of conservative nationalism: writing in dialect. The supporters of dialect did not accept the design of the unified Basque language, *Euskara batua*, which was violently opposed from several corners. In the charged atmosphere of the time, the controversy ended in the complete victory of the position in favor of *Euskara batua* that Aresti defended.

His cultural commitment was enriched by his dedication to writing for the theater, theatrical performance, and collaboration with a number of singers in the Basque Country, most prominently his work with the Bilbao group Oskorri between 1972 and 1975, which popularized Aresti's reputation and writing.

To conclude this section, in his socially conscious poetry, Gabriel Aresti gave voice to the impulses for social and political renewal of a new, anti-Franco Basque society with socialist leanings that would burst into view in the spring of 1968, with various front lines of social mobilization: in Paris, in Czechoslovakia, on the streets of San Francisco, and in California's universities. His work extended across multiple literary genres. He wrote plays, novels, and short stories, but his renown comes fundamentally from the popularity among readers of his three books of socially conscious poetry, the first of which was *Harri eta herri* (1964).

Gabriel Aresti between Two Aesthetics: From Symbolism to Social Consciousness

The two books included in this publication, *Maldan behera* (*Downhill*, 1960) and *Harri eta herri* (*Rock & Core*, 1964), correspond to two different periods in Gabriel Aresti's poetry and two different conceptions of poetry itself. The former is a symbolist cycle, while the latter is fully committed to a poetry of social consciousness.

Basque conservative nationalism, the ideological and linguistic components of which we have described in the first section, also included an aesthetic position that originated in the period prior to the 1936 Spanish Civil War. Between 1930 and 1936, there was a great explosion of Basque lyric. Three authors, Nicolás Ormatxea, known as Orixe (1888–1961), José María Agirre, who wrote as Xabier de Lizardi (1896–1933), and Esteban Urkiaga, known as Lauaxeta (1905–1937), revitalized Basque poetry. The latter two worked in a lyric style that followed in the footsteps of the French symbolists and the early-twentieth-century Spanish writers of the beginning of the century, from Miguel Unamuno (1864–1936) to Antonio Machado (1875–1939) and the early Juan Ramón Jiménez (1881–1954), and the authors of Spain's Generation of 1927, with special attention to Federico García Lorca (1898–1936) and Rafael Alberti (1902–1999) in the case of Esteban Urkiaga, Lauxeta. Among the three, Xabier de Lizardi, long considered the greatest Basque lyric poet, enjoyed great prestige. His work and his symbolist aesthetics were held up throughout the entire post–civil war period as a model worthy of admiration and imitation. Like all the symbolists, Lizardi opted for metaphor as a fundamental mode of poetic communication, highlighted the ideal as a fundamental element that had to be attained, and created a poetry that used the description of nature as the basis for its central message of the passage of time and the finitude of human existence. From the late 1930s until well into the 1960s, the hegemonic current of Basque poetry directed its footsteps along the same path that Lizardi had followed: metaphor, idealism, and a certain existential sense, with a poetic diction that made use of meter and rhyme, almost never free verse, and drew on popular aesthetics in its use of song forms, but distanced itself from what it considered to be the vulgar production of the *bertsolariak*, rural oral improvisers.

Aresti was no stranger to what was going on around him, and even if he drew on the forms of the *bertsolariak* from the beginning, he later called for a symbolist poetry influenced by the great symbolist poets of the pre–civil war (Lizardi and Juan de Arana, known as Loramendi, 1907–1933) and post–civil war (Jean Diharce, known as Iratzeder, 1920–2008) periods, but precisely in order to exhaust it, from a perspective that would take this symbolist current to its extreme limits. *Maldan behera* (1960) was the fruit of this effort.

The poet described his intention in a letter he sent to the Prague philologist Norbert Tauer (1898–1983) in December 1959, apparently after having already completed the great work of poetry that is *Maldan behera*:

> *Badakizu lehen poesiak idazten nituela. Lizardiri eta gaurko beste olerkariari imitatzen nien, baina egun batean haien idaztankera etzaidan jatorra iruditu eta bertsolariek nola egiten duten, eta nola egin zuten behinolako poetek estudiatzen paratu nintzen. Handik beste bat atera nintzen. Ikusi dut poesi jator eta usariodun bat dagoela eta hari lotu natzaio* (Aresti 1986, 140–41).
>
> [You know that I used to write poems. I imitated Lizardi and other contemporary poets, but one day it seemed to me that their writings were not sincere, and I set out to study how the *bertsolariak*[3] and the old poets did it. I came away from that a different person. I have seen that another, sincere and traditional poetry exists, and I want to unite myself to it.]

---

3. *Bertsolari*: a poet who improvises his verses with the support of a traditional sung meter. The form is the chief expression of Basque oral literature. For more information, see Samuel G. Armistead and Joseba Zulaika, eds. *Voicing the Moment: Improvised Oral Poetry and Basque Tradition* (Reno: Center for Basque Studies, University of Nevada, Reno, 2005), Joxe Mallea-Olaetxe, *Shooting from the Lip: Improvised Basque-Verse Singing* (Reno: NABO, 2002), or go to the website www.bertsozale.eus.

This reference to Lizardi and contemporary poets can mean only the symbolist poets who are clearly cited in the titles of the poems found in *Maldan behera*, among whom Aresti included himself, as the final link in a chain that was about to come to an end due to its "lack of sincerity."

In February of the same year, in a letter written in Spanish to Txomin Peillen (1932–), a Basque writer living in Paris and known for his heterodoxy and secularism, Aresti confessed his admiration for his fellow Bilbao poet Blas de Otero (1916–1979):

> I have finished ruminating on Blas de Otero's *Ancia*. This Otero is a colossus, the best poet in Spanish since Salinas died . . . The way Otero goes along distilling his poison, getting around ecclesiastical and political censorship, is something to marvel at . . . He has now melded the first two [books, *Ángel fieramente humano* (Fiercely human angel) and *Redoble de conciencia* (Drumbeat of conscience)] together in *Ancia* . . . which I have no clue what it means, but perhaps it's *Hacia* [Toward] as they pronounce it in Castile (Aresti 1986, 134–35).

Aresti's preference for Pedro Salinas (1891–1951) and his love poetry is well known. Now, Blas de Otero, a poet who would open the door for Aresti's change in aesthetics, appears chronologically after Salinas. From Otero, Aresti would derive a change in poetry's meaning, from a poetry of metaphor and symbol to one of clear speaking and blasphemy, as he wrote in his letter to Txomin Peillen: "He is thinking about ultimately melding *Ancia* together with *Con la inmensa mayoría* [With the vast majority] in order to put forward a final work, the name of which he has not yet chosen, but which will be so anti-poetic that it will sound like a blasphemy, and he says that his poetic work will then be that word" (Aresti 1986, 135).

From the poetry of symbols to anti-poetry or the poetry of blasphemy, a poetry of direct speaking. In the letter we have been discussing, Aresti already described some of Otero's techniques that he would use in *Harri eta herri* (1964), the second book published in this volume.

Each of the two books thus corresponds to a different aesthetic conception: first, the acceptance of symbolist presuppositions; second, the expression of social consciousness by means of anti-poetry. They bring together poetry of daily life that knows how to take wing while "getting around ecclesiastical or political censorship."

In Basque studies of Aresti, it is said that the poet took this step after being disappointed by the failure that met *Maldan behera*'s publication—a relative failure in any event, since it won the Loramendi Prize in September 1959. It was published in the journal *Euskera*, the official organ of the Academy of the Basque Language,[4] which sponsored the prize. The fact that it was published in a journal did not help its distribution, and Aresti in fact wanted to add another section to the text (a second part, which we do not have) and publish it in book form, a project that did not come to fruition.

What is certain, however, is that starting from Otero's realistic and socially conscious aesthetics, Aresti was advancing toward the creation of a socially conscious and ideological aesthetics of his own, which would come to fruition in *Zuzenbide debekatua* (Justice under interdict, 1961, still unfinished in February but submitted for a prize in May, although Aresti sent a copy to Joxe Azurmendi in April), a work that could not be published due to its extremely harsh denunciation of the social situation under Franco and was little known until Professor Karmelo Landa edited it in 1986. The poem arose out of that conception of social consciousness and probably had two immediate sparks: the murder of Javier Batarrita at a Civil Guard checkpoint, for which no one was held responsible, in March 1961 (Santarén 2014) and the detention and torture of Gabriel del Moral, released from prison in July of the same year, about which Aresti wrote an elegy, "Lamento por la prisión de Gabriel Moral Zabala" (Lament for Gabriel Moral Zabala's imprisonment, Aresti 1986c, 111–13).

For this reason, we should suppose that Aresti's rechanneling of his energies in the direction of socially conscious poetry arose out of an awareness that was capable of uniting serious aesthetic reflection, conducted in the wake of his reading of Otero, with social indignation created by the injustice he saw in society and symbolized by the harsh and tragic events of which his friends were victims.

Maldan behera

Gabriel Aresti's first major work is titled *Maldan behera* (*Downhill*, 1960). The subtitle is *Miren eta Joaneren historiaren bukaera* (The End of Miren and Joan's Story). It is a grand symbolist poem in which multiple lines of signification intersect. As we have seen previously, the Bilbao poet said that he had been inspired by the works of Xabier de Lizardi and "other contemporary poets" in bringing it to fruition.

---

4. Institution responsible for safeguarding Basque linguistic norms, created in 1919. It promotes studies of the Basque language in the areas of dialectology, lexicography, and grammar. Further information can be found at www.euskaltzaindia.net.

The overall plot is easy to describe: *Maldan behera* recounts a journey out of the mountains by a prophetic Ego, a superman. This initiation takes him through four stages (the oak forest, the ash forest, the field of ferns, and the meadow of flowers, referring to four Basque poets, Aresti, Lizardi, Iratzeder, and Loramendi, the last three symbolists), along paths that are more modern each time: the footpath, the sunken lane, the cart track, the road. This prophet wants to awaken the apes from their subhuman situation, in which they are living in miserable conditions that can be interpreted as the alienated life of Basque society under Franco. The apes do not listen to him, and they kill Joan and Miren, crucifying them back to back on a single cross. The prophet is judged, crucified, and buried. Miren comes back to life, and later, so does Joan. The second part of the poem recounts an ascent through various states of consciousness—rest, hatred, adoration, desire, and joy—in a sequence of acts that lead Joan to take vengeance on those who killed him. The superman punishes the apes and returns to the mountains with Miren, leaving the apes in their situation of poverty. He does not deign to liberate them again, and the poem ends with the lovers' embrace.

Much has been written about the symmetrical aspects of this long symbolist poem, a symmetry that appears not only in its structure, but also in its metrical framework: Aresti uses a different stanzaic pattern in each of the poem's major sequences, in addition to paying deliberate attention to the numbers involved. The poem has two parts, almost two thousand lines (1,916, to be precise), and 222 stanzas, but Aresti indicated that each part is made up of 677 rhymes. Coming from an accountant who gave a symbolic character to the numbers in a short story, this numerical reference is more than a professional reflex: it turns out to be the search for a symbol. Probably, "677" indicates an overcoming of the cursed number "666," the number of the beast. The work begins with four quotations, from Nietzsche's *Thus Spoke Zarathustra*, the Gospels, T. S. Eliot, and Salinas.

Ibon Sarasola (1979) interprets the poem as having a double meaning: it recounts the Superman's journey through the history of Basque poetry, by way of the mention of the four poets already noted, and a descent from the mountains to the city in a civilizing process that leads from the footpath to the highway.[5] Consequently, it seems that it is si-

5. The nom-de-plumes (Aresti, Lizardi, Iratzeder, and Loramendi) do, in fact, literally refer to the four stages (oak, ash, fern, flower): *aresti* means "oak forest"; *lizardi* means "ash grove"; *iratzeder* means "beautiful fern"; and *loramendi* means "mountain of flowers" or "flower(y) mountain."

multaneously a poem of decline, since there is a descent, and one of progress, since there is forward movement, a juxtaposition that Sarasola does not discuss. This contradiction is noticed by Jon Juaristi (1987, 26), who argues that the movement toward the city parallels the scheme proposed by Lewis Mumford for the stages of urban development, from eopolis through polis, metropolis, megalopolis, and tyrannopolis to necropolis, while indicating that in the poem, Aresti moves directly from the polis to the necropolis. Underlining another symmetry, the poem begins in a desert and ends its first part in a cemetery.

The crucial problem with Sarasola's interpretation is that he only analyzes the titles of the first part and leaves the analysis of the second part untouched. Unitary readings of the poem have been carried out by both Aurelia Arkotxa (1993) and Iñaki Aldekoa (1998). In his study, the latter scholar highlights the importance of Dante, the Bible, and Unamuno in the poem's configuration. He traces its symbols to *The Waste Land* (1922) by T. S. Eliot (1888–1965) and the symbolic interpretation of *The Golden Bough* (1922) by James George Frazer (1854–1941). Where Eliot's influence is concerned, Basque scholars have emphasized the parallels between *Maldan behera* and *The Waste Land*, since the Basque poem begins with its protagonist in a barren land.

Sebastián García Trujillo, in a still-unpublished study, proposes a double reading that nuances and completes some of those that have been put forward up to now. First, he emphasizes, with support from Aresti's subsequent work, that Joan is the namesake of John the Baptist (as Aresti himself had noted and as Aldekoa stresses). According to this author, the Joan of *Maldan behera* has clear parallels to John the Baptist and to Jesus, especially in the passages about the crucifixion. Nevertheless, the characteristics of the violence against the apes do not fit this model, but can be ascribed to Nietzsche's Zarathustra.

Aresti indicated that the work was intended to be a love poem, explaining the reference to Salinas, little explored by Basque criticism:

> I've half given up on the Ballads [*Coplario*] of Miren, which is the last thing that I'm missing in order to finish my poem. You may not be familiar with its trajectory. You already know how I wrote *Maldan behera* in order to introduce myself to Loramendi. *Maldan behera* is not a complete poem in itself; it's fragmentary. For this reason, I later wrote *Azkenengo besarkada* [Last embrace], which could very well have been called *Malden gora*, although I initially baptized it *Miren eta Joane*. Between the two, Joan's vision was reasonably well explained. But Miren was missing. Love cannot be

> egotistical; in every dispute, both sides have to be heard. For this reason, I decided to explain Miren's participation in the matter, and I conceived the Ballads, *Mirenen koplategia* [Miren's book of ballads], which will go in between the other two (1986d, 140).

Nothing apparently remains of this work in progress, at least in the form in which Aresti described it, although he would later use the title *Miren eta Joaneren historiaren hasiera* (The beginning of the story of Miren and Joan) for a work different in content from the one mentioned here. The poem's biographical basis cannot be left out of consideration. If it is a love poem, Aresti brings to it his breakup with his nationalist fiancée, which led to his expulsion from that community, and his encounter with the new Eve in the figure of Meli Esteban. At root, it is the same story he recounted in *Bizkaitarra* (The Bizkaian, The nationalist), a cycle of five poems that preceded *Maldan behera*, but with a key difference: the earlier poems are written in the popular meter used by the *bertsolariak*. *Maldan behera* uses a meter similar to the poetic language of Lizardi, who conceived one of his most famous poems as an ascent into the mountains. Aresti's descent is a backhanded allusion to this poem by Lizardi.

If it is accepted that Aresti's poem deals with the end of a relationship, the subtitle ("The end of the story") can be read as referring to a relationship that has ended, leading to a descent, but which the new Eve will convert into resurrection and a return to the mountains. In addition, however, Aresti was concerned with a different topic at this time: the arrival of a Messiah who could change the direction of the Basque people's social history. In effect, three of the quotations placed at the beginning of the poem, the one from Nietzsche, the one from the Gospels, and especially the one from T. S. Eliot, highlight a figure who is capable of giving his life for the salvation of the community. Where the relationship between T. S. Eliot and Aresti is concerned, the importance of *The Waste Land*'s influence has been studied without recognizing that this quotation comes not from this work, but from *Murder in the Cathedral* (1935), and in this regard, Thomas Becket's death in Canterbury Cathedral in 1170 can be seen as parallel to that of Jesus. Aresti thus shapes a messianic figure, a complex of associations surrounding a superior being who wants to save a people and is rejected by them. Like Becket, like Jesus, like Aresti himself.

Harri eta herri

This book of poems brought Gabriel Aresti wide recognition in the field of Basque poetry. It is beyond question that, even if sales were modest, it was a book devoured by young people and new writers who saw in Aresti's *dictum* a new aesthetics that drew its material from a time of change.

Harri eta herri is a response to the aesthetics that Aresti learned from Blas de Otero's poetry, a socially conscious, direct poetry that breaks with purism and seeks anti-poetry, a diction in which the lines are directly and clearly comprehensible, direct, and clear. It is at times blasphemous and always far removed from symbolist aestheticism, although this does not mean that there are no symbols in the text.

In the title, the play on words between *harri*, "stone," and *herri*, "people," "town," or "country" attracts attention. A people of stone, an imposing barricade against Franco's regime, an indomitable will. There are various interpretations of this ingenious homonymy and identification between stone and people. The first sees a reference to prehistory, the Stone Age, in which Jorge Oteiza (1908–2003) located a golden age of Basque art (Oteiza 1983), alongside Fr. Joxe Migel Barandiaran's (1889–1991) research into the prehistoric period.[6] The second discerns traces of the texts of Miguel Hernández (1910–1942), who spoke of "Basques armored in stone," or the Galician poet Celso Emilio Ferreiro's (1912–1979) *Longa noite de pedra* (Long night of stone), a title intended to name the long night of Franco's regime, or the impression made on Aresti by his contemplation of the stones of the hermitage of Salbatore in Abadiño, Bizkaia, where twelve stones represent twelve towns (Zelaieta 2000, 82).

It is an encompassing title for a book that, according to its subtitle (unfortunately absent in the 1969 second edition and in Karmelo Landa's good 1986 edition), is a collection of "ballads [*coplas*], popular improvisations [*bertsos*], sayings [*dichos*], and poems," that is, a union of four distinct poetic genres. This is a key to the work that is very rarely mentioned, because this subtitle demonstrates that Aresti had in mind a work that brings together diverse elements, characteristic of a poetics centered on immediate experience. Joxe Azurmendi (1985) has described the configuration of Aresti's poetry as "a concrete sensibility,"

6. Interested readers in English can consult Jorge Oteiza, *Oteiza's Selected Writings* (Reno: Center for Basque Studies, 2003) and José Miguel de Barandiaran, *Selected Writings of José Miguel Barandiarán: Basque Prehistory and Ethnography* (Reno: Center for Basque Studies, 2007).

one that from observation of daily life is able to arrive at symbolism, a metaphor of daily life from the perspective of formal variety and the diversity found in observation of the real and the everyday.

This poetic conception owes much to Aresti's reading of Blas de Otero and to a change in his aesthetic perception. Already in 1959, Aresti wrote that he was reading and "ruminating on" Otero's *Ancia*.

A few months earlier, as well, in a letter to Txomin Peillen, Aresti summarized in the word "blasphemy" the poetic form that he wanted for his poetry.

And not long after, explicit reference to "blasphemy" appeared in his poetry:

> *Birao egiten zuten./Okerbideak ezpaitaki mintzaerarik,/berdin tratatzen baitu/erdalduna/eta/euskalduna* (1986b, 17).

> They swore,/because injustice is no polyglot/and treats/Castilian/and Basque/equally (1986b, 16).

This new poetic attitude led Aresti to pay attention to the situation of the people who lived around him. In the four parts into which the book is divided, Aresti draws a map of the injustices society suffered under Franco's policies.

Harri eta herri was born out of a twofold poetic movement. First, Aresti looked out and around at the unjust situations produced in society, giving his poetry a narrative character; second, the poet turned inward to construct a coherent and comprehensive image of his "poetic self" as a poet-prophet who will always speak the truth and who will defend justice.

The book's four sections have different poetic accents. In the first section, Blas de Otero's influence is clear: the poems recount the stories of people who may or may not have a relationship to Aresti. The narrative tone and the presence of different characters give the poems the flavor of parables manifesting the injustices of society under Franco. Soon, however, in this same section, Aresti presents a definition of himself as the measure of the world and in terms of a strict identification between being and speaking: a poet is a poet to the extent that he speaks the truth, and speaking the truth is enough to create poetry. This "I" who protests and speaks the truth in the name of justice thus comes from a reading of Walt Whitman, whose presence very quickly makes an appearance in the poetic text: Whitman's "Song of Myself" and his "I exist as I am" are two important axes around which Aresti will create his poetry.

The second section of the book presents a dialogue with tradition. If irony and shifting registers mark the style of the first part, self-citation and reflection on traditional creation punctuate a section in which traditional diction is opened up. Aresti's famous poem "Nire aitaren etxea" (My father's house) is found in this section.

The third part is structured around two axes: condemnation of money as a corruptor of society and reflection on poetry in a long poem dedicated to the sculptor Jorge Oteiza, in which the poet defends his clear poetry, distanced from that of the vanguard.

The fourth section uses the figure of Aresti's paternal grandfather to take up once more the story of an individual distanced from society and the myth of regeneration through the arrival of a messianic prophet who will change the world. This long narrative poem probably returns to some of the complexes of meaning that Aresti had developed in his symbolist period.

From its topics to its diction, *Harri eta herri* brought about a profound renewal of Basque poetry, locating it in history, in the history of modernity, and in a harsh critique of society under Franco.

Thanksgivings

From symbolism to the poetry of social consciousness, Gabriel Aresti's work is considered one of the turning points in the history of Basque literature. For this reason, it is cause for gratitude that it is being included in this collection of Basque classics published by the William A. Douglass Center for Basque Studies at the University of Nevada, Reno with the assistance of the Bizkaiko Foru Aldundia-Diputación Foral de Bizkaia.

In addition, it repairs a forgotten injustice. In 1961, Gabriel Aresti wrote that the great educator Koldo Mitxelena had asked him for a selection of poems from his *Zuzenbide debekatua* (1961), then still unfinished, in order to publish them with the University of Texas at Austin. To the best of my knowledge, the initiative went no further, although the matter has not been thoroughly researched.

That first attempt at publication with an American university press now finds a fortunate successor in the William A. Douglass Center for Basque Studies edition, and we are certain that it will serve to make Gabriel Aresti's profound poetry better known.

Bibliography

Aresti, Gabriel. 1976. *Obra Guztiak: Poemak I-II*. Edited by Jon Juaristi. Donostia: Kriselu.

———. 1986a. *Gabriel Arestiren Literatur Lanak -1: Lehen poesiak*. Edited by Karmelo Landa. Zarautz: Susa.

———. 1986b. *Gabriel Arestiren Literatur Lanak -2: Harri eta Herri*. Zarautz: Susa.

———. 1986c. *Gabriel Arestiren Literatur Lanak -5: Poesia argitaragabea: Azken poesia*. Zarautz: Susa.

———. 1986d. *Gabriel Arestiren Literatur Lanak -10: Artikuluak: Hitz-aldiak: Gutunak*. Edited by Karmelo Landa. Zarautz: Susa.

Aldekoa, Iñaki. 1993. *Zirkuluaren hutsmina*. Irun: Alberdania.

———. 1998. "Gabriel Arestiren Maldan Behera." *Anuario Seminario Julio de Urquijo* 32 (2): 435–510.

Arkotxa, Aurelia. 1993. "Imaginaire et poésie dans Maldan behera de Gabriel Aresti (1933–1975)." *Anuario Seminario Julio de Urquijo* (1993). Accessed June 2016. www.ehu.es/ojs/index.php/ASJU/article/download/8183/7329.

Armistead, Samuel G., and Joseba Zulaika, eds. 2005. *Voicing the Moment: Improvised Oral Poetry and Basque Tradition*. Reno: Center for Basque Studies, University of Nevada, Reno.

Atxaga, Bernardo. 2000. "Aresti eta bere inguru zaila." In *Gabriel Aresti (1933-1975): Gabriel Arestiren mundua: Erakusketa eta Jardunaldiak*, 43–60. Bilb
o: Bilboko Udala-Gipuzkoako Foru Aldundia.

Azurmendi, Joxe. 1985. "Aresti: Sentsibilitate konkretu bat." *Jakin* 36: 5–30.

Barandiaran, José Miguel de. *Selected Writings of José Miguel Barandiarán: Basque Prehistory and Ethnography*. Reno: Center for Basque Studies, 2007.

Begiarmen. 1974. *Sei idazle plazara*. Oñati: Jakin.

Cadarso, Honorio. 2001. "En torno a Gabriel Aresti: Geografía sentimental de un poeta bilbaíno." *Bidebarrieta* 9: 81–103.

Del Cerro, Rakel, and Juan Carlos Romera. 2001. "Gabriel Aresti, izena eta izana." *Bidebarrieta* 9: 17–80.

Juaristi, Jon. 1976. "Hitzatze/Epílogo." In Gabriel Aresti, *Obra Guztiak: Poemak II*, 506–17. Donostia: Kriseilu.

———. 1987. *Historia de la literatura vasca*. Madrid: Taurus.

Kintana, Xabier, ed. 2014. *Harri eta Herri: Artikulu Bilduma*. Bilbao: Euskaltzaindia; Gabriel Aresti Kultura Elkartea.

Kortazar, Jon. 2003. *El poeta Gabriel Aresti (1933–1975)*. Bilbao: Fundación BBK.

——. 2010. "El poeta Gabriel Aresti." *Cuadernos de Alzate* 43: 68–101.

Laka, Itziar. 1987. "Manuel Arriandaga: Berrazterketarako oinarriak (Hiperbizkaiaren historiaz)." *Anuario del Seminario de Filología Vasca Julio de Urquijo* 21 (3): 727–53. Accessed June 2016. http://www.ehu.es/ojs/index.php/ASJU/article/view/7935.

Landa, Karmelo. 1999. "Gabriel Arestiren obra." In *Gabriel Arestiri Omenaldia: Bilbok bere seme prestuari: 1986ko Ihardunaldien aktak*, 35–48. Bilbao: Bilboko Udala.

——. 2013. "Gabriel Aresti: Nazionalismoa eta Sozialismoa Bilbon eta Euskal Herrian." In Elkar Lanean, *Bilbon, 2012ko irailaren 14an egindako Nazionalismoa ikertuz: Nazionalismoa, demokrazia eta kultura I. Kongresuaren akta-liburua/Minutes Book of Research on Nationalism 1st Conference: Nationalism, Democracy and Culture: Bilbao, September 14th, 2012*, 113–22. Bilbao: Euskal Herriko Uniberstitatea.

Lasa, Mikel. 1964. "Harri eta Herri." *Egan*, 161–63.

Lekuona, Juan Mari. 1970. "Aozko poesia eta olerki uain berria." *Zeruko Argia*, Azaroak 1.3.

Mallea-Olaetxe, Joxe. 2002. *Shooting from the Lip: Improvised Basque-Verse Singing*. Reno: NABO.

Mitxelena, Koldo. 1978. "Miscelania filológica vasca II: Aspectos de la métrica de Aresti." *Fontes Linguae Vasconum* 10: 389–413.

Nanclares Gómez, Gustavo. 1998. *Tras el reino de piedra: Una aproximación a la literatura nacionalista vasca y gallega de los años 60*. Vitoria-Gasteiz: Diputación Foral de Alava.

Oteiza, Jorge. 1983. *Ejercicios espirituales en un túnel*. Donostia: Hordago.

——. *Oteiza's Selected Writings*. Edited by Joseba Zulaika. Reno: Center for Basque Studies, 2003.

Salaburu, Pello, ed. 2008. *Koldo Mitxelena: Selected Writings of a Basque Scholar*. Reno: Center for Basque Studies, University of Nevada, Reno.

——. 2015. *Writing Words: The Unique Case of the Standardization of Basque*. Reno: Center for Basque Studies, University of Nevada, Reno.

Salaburu, Pello, and Xabier Alberdi, eds. 2012. *The Challenge of a Bilingual Society in the Basque Country*. Reno: Center for Basque Studies, University of Nevada, Reno.

San Martin, Juan. 1964. "Aintzin-Solasa." In Gabriel Aresti, *Harri eta herri*. Zarautz: Itxaropena.

Santaren, Enrique. 2014. "Batarrita, 49 tiros en una ejecución policial por error." *Deia* (April 6).

Sarasola, Ibon. 1979. "Hitzaurrea." In Gabriel Aresti, *Obra guztiak: Poemak I*, 10–99. Donostia: Haranburu Altuna.

Various authors. 1999. *Gabriel Arestiri Omenaldia: Bilbok bere seme prestuari: 1986ko Ihardunaldien aktak*. Bilbao: Bilboko Udala.

Various authors. 2000. *Gabriel Aresti (1933-1975): Gabriel Arestiren mundua: Erakusketa eta Jardunaldiak*. Bilbo; Donostia: Bilboko Udala; Gipuzkoako Foru Aldundia.

Zelaieta, Angel. 1976. *Gabriel Aresti*. Donostia: Kriselu. Second edition, 2000. Zarautz: Susa.

EDITORIAL NOTE

Throughout the text, certain places, concepts, and other things relating to Basque culture that deserve further explanation have been marked with an asterisk (*). Interested readers will find explanatory notes regarding these, organized by page number, at the end of the book.

DOWNHILL

(Maldan behera)

The End of Miren and Joan's Story

(Miren eta Joaneren historiaren bukaera)

Ich gebe kein Almosen. Dazu bin ich nicht arm genug.
— Friedrich Nietzsche, *Also Sprach Zarathustra*

Ego sum vitis, vos palmites.
— *Biblia Sacra Vulgata*, Joannem XV

There is no danger for us, and there is no safety in the Cathedral.
— T. S. Eliot, *Murder in the Cathedral*

Estoy al borde mismo de tu sueño.
— Pedro Salinas, *Razón de amor*

Jean Miranderi and Gabino Arestiri

I. Untergang

Egun honetan nire gogoak
utzi nai baitu mendia,
MALDAN BEHERA DOA AGURO
NIRE GORPUTZ BILUZIA.

Honera etorri baino leen ongi
ezautu nuen herria;
txiki-denporan eduki nuen
han ene bizitegia.
Ama maiteak emaro niri
ematen zidan ditia:
MALDAN BEHERA DOA AGURO
NIRE GORPUTZ BILUZIA.

Honera ekarri nuen handikan
nire tristura haundia,
gizon doilorrek egin zidaten
bidegabe itsusia.
Orain zikina, zitala banaiz
orduan nintzen garbia:
MALDAN BEHERA DOA AGURO
NIRE GORPUTZ BILUZIA.

To Jon Mirande and Gabino Aresti

I. Untergang

Because my spirit today
wants to flee the mountain
DOWNHILL FAST
MY NAKED BODY GOES.

Before I came here
I knew the village well;
in my child-time
this was home,
and mom was love,
as was her breast always:
DOWNHILL FAST
MY NAKED BODY GOES.

From back there I carried
my great sadness along,
evil men laid down
traps for me to fall.
All innocence I once had gone,
now I'm filth and aim low.
DOWNHILL FAST
MY NAKED BODY GOES.

Mendi gailurrak ikusi zidan
arduraz penitentzia,
haranerantza ibilkeko
eman zidan lizentzia;
hari entzunik dirudit orain
hegaztina kantaria:
MALDAN BEHERA DOA AGURO
NIRE GORPUTZ BILUZIA.

II. Hariztia

Orain hemen nago, eremu latz honetan.
Nire gurariak galdurik, lur hauetan
arbola adar-gabeen parea naiz orain.
Landare zekenak baitaduzka eremuak,
erratzak harean, haitzetan kalamuak,
nire arima dago mirari baten zain.

Eztago zeruan egun hodei batere.
Denpora sikuak garantzen ditu bere
ordu miragarriak sekula batean.
Zerura begira egoten naiz luzaro,
izarren esnetik edaten dut oparo,
baina egarri bizia daukat bihotzean.

Azken eremuon natzalako atinik,
hezur-lekuetan eztaukat zer-eginik,
ta iruten dut astiro itogin sikua,
nundik egunotan doakidan bihotza,
entzun eztelako ur lasterraren hotsa,
apur bat busti dezan lurreko kolkua.

Eztut gaur ezer jan: eztut horren beharrik;
eta gau osoan egondu naiz itzarrik,
kandeletan ikisiz eulien hegalak.
Barauetan eztut oinazerik aurkitu,
bakarrik egoteko asmotxo makalak,
eta lo-gelak benedikatu ditu.

The mountain peaks
sensed my need for penitence
and gave me license
to walk into the valley;
as I listen to their song
I feel bird and I sing too:
DOWNHILL FAST
MY NAKED BODY GOES

II. The Oakwood

Now I'm here, in this wasteland,
all hope gone from this barren plain,
branchless tree I am, un-windswept.
Gaunt plants inhabit this desert,
roots in sand, fragile stems in rock,
likewise my soul awaits miracles too.

Not a single cloud in the sky.
Dry-time slides across the blue
in eternal hours of wonder.
I stare at the sky forever,
gulp down star-milk by the gallon,
and my heart remains thirsty.

Looking up lying down on the last horizon
I see there'll be no ossuary for me,
and it feels like a slow dry drip,
how my heart vanishes bit by bit,
because I can't hear the rapids
wet the throat of the earth below.

I haven't eaten today: I don't need to;
and was awake all night, watching
the wings of flies float in the candle wax.
The fast does me no harm,
my encompassing wish is to be alone,
and this blessed room complies.

Eremuek ere dauzkalako mareak,
behera eta gora egiten du hareak,
eta nire gorputzak ezin egon zutik.
Arroken ostean agertu den etsaia
ene begian da baratzeko galaia,
itsuki baitiotsat: Ken hadi hemendik!

Haitz gorri beltzetik datorren arranoak
moldegaizki lotzen dizkit anka-besoak,
eta laket bizian etzaten da lotan.
Koba sakonetik irten duen sugeak
egunero dizkit moztutzen bost erpeak;
hegaztinari zaio hurbiltzen narrastan.

Batzutan diotsat ilunpeko jaunari:
pozetan negarrez, doloretan kantari,
gizona zen emazte urrikaria nauk,
nire ezpainetan dagoen ur gazia
oraintxe kentzeko, egin zaidak grazia;
ezin paira nitzake premia gogor hauk.

Animali biok dira nire lagunak;
nire deserriko nahats geza bigunak,
ze moduz jakin gabe, orain dizkiet zor.
Biziko lorean ernatu da kimua:
Sugea, arranoa, ta azkenean zimua;
hiru animalia baizik eztago hor.

Gainerakoa da alperrikako gauza:
hermita eroria, hobietako lauza:
eta maitalearen gorputz usteldua;
ezpaitzekidaten benetan erantzuten,
mugitu ezineko itxura hartu zuten
herio geldiaren mustur zimeldua.

Gauerdi batekin agertu zen arraina,
zilarrezko ezkatak eta buztan apaina:
Eznuen konprenitu nundik etorri zen.
Goizaldean, noski, paratu zen marean,
ta gero sartu zen jarri nion sarean,
iheri neuganantza ahalik lasterren.

Because the desert also has tides,
like the sea sand goes up, down . . .
so much so my body can't stand.
An enemy emerges from the rocks,
it's in my eye, an oasis offering rest,
and stubborn I request: go away, go away!

The eagle glides from rocks red and black
to clumsily tie up my legs and my arms,
then folds in happy for a sweet nap.
The serpent slides out of its deep cave
and daily removes my fingers one by one;
then zigzags a path back to the fowl.

Sometimes I tell the god of darkness:
in joy, in tears, as I sing in pain,
I am your pious wife who was once man,
take the salt from my lips right now,
please grant me that grace,
I can't survive this relentless grief.

Both animals are my friends,
the soft first grapes of my exile;
I owe them, somehow, not sure how.
A seedling sprouts from the flower of life:
the snake, the eagle, and the chimp alive;
nothing here other than three forms of life.

The rest is the void:
the crumbling hermitage, the gaping tomb,
and the rotting lover's corpse;
none could ever truly answer me
and thus ended paralyzed, still,
with lips withered in death's grip.

The fish arrived in the middle of the night,
all silver scales and magnificent tail:
I didn't understand its provenance.
With dawn, of course, with the tide,
it swam into the net I laid
and toward me, eager, fast.

Bere aginekin eman zidan dolore,
kolore denetan: gorri, beilegi, more,
ikusten bainizkion begi biribilak,
gutiziarekin, bere hegal zimelak
ebaki zizkidan tenorean kordelak,
geldiro libraturik nire orkatilak.

Eta indarrarekin eman zuen bizia.
Nire sabelean mendekuzko zuzia
izar baten moduan izeki zitzaidan.
Nire etsaiak zeuden lekurantza joan nintzen;
biak nituen hil, eta eguzki-brintzen
edertasun zabala argitu zen nigan.

Hiru gorputzekin egin nuen arbola
sukuari, gero, eman nion odola,
bihotzetik ugari atera nuena.
Arrainen hagalak ziren bere sustarrak,
arrano zuren lumak ziren adarrak,
eta bere tronkua sugeen buztana.

Haritz bedeinkatua
adoratu nuen.
Nire belaunak
lurrean jarri
nituen.
Ordu hartan
nik eznenkien
zerk iharrosi
ninduen.
Haritz bedeinkatua
adoratu nuen.

Arbola bakarreko
harizti maitea:
Egun oraindik
eztutu bete
urtea;
indar haundiz
apurtu duzu
lotu ninduen
katea.

It hurt me with its teeth, my pain
was yellow, purple, red: every shade,
I could see its rounded eyes well;
knifelike, then its sharp fins
cut through the ropes and
freed up my ankles seamlessly.

And its force gave me life,
lit the torch of revenge in my entrails,
became the star I carried inside.
So I went to my enemies
and killed them both, and let the sun
fill me, spark me up with light.

With the three corpses I made a tree
which I fed with the blood that
from them flowed profusely.
The fish's fins were roots,
the eagle's wings added branches,
the snake's body was its trunk.

This holy oak*
I adored.
My knees
hit
the soil.
I still don't know
what strange power
compelled me
to my core.
I adored
this holy oak.

My beloved
one-tree Oakwood:
not
a year old
yet.
With what force
you broke
the chain
that bound me.

Arbola bakarreko
harizti maitea.
Haritzaren adarrak
mugituz biziro,
aita nirea
balitz bezala
emaro,
behar nuen
bendizioa
partitu zidan
luzaro.
Haritzaren adarrak
mugituz biziro.

Horko bidea gaitza dela,
ezta kamino zabala.
Harri zorrotzak daude hortik, minduko zaitzu oin-zola
Basamortua,
arantz-ortua,
laga zazu berehala.

Etorri zinen haranetik
estrata luze batetik:
Orain zu zara itzuliko gauza guztiak utzirik,
lehengo estrata
itzali da-ta,
bide-zihor horretatik.

Frutu gozorik ezpaituzu
mendi honetan dastatu,
agi garratz bat behar dizut bene-benetan aitortu:
gaueko izotzak
aratz zorrotzak
metxiketan sartu ditu.

Udaberriko gau ederra
bihurtu zaigu gogorra;
elur zuriak estali du hemengo mendigailurra,
ta krabelina,
apain ta fina,
orain ezta mundutarra.

My beloved
one-tree Oakwood.
The oak spread
its branches
open, vigorous,
it was
like my father
gave the blessing
I longed for
and spoke, solemn, slow,
magnanimous.
The oak spread
its branches
open, vigorous.

Know that the road is tough
and the path narrow.
That sharp stones abound and your soles will hurt:
Leave now
this barren soil,
this land of thorns.

You came from the valley,
followed a long path:
go back now,
leave everything behind,
know the harsh old road
no longer stands.

No sweet fruits to taste
in this mountain,
the bitter truth, I must confess
is that night frost
stabbed needles
into the apricots.

The beautiful spring night
turned raw and hard,
snow covered the caps,
and carnations,
so pretty and fine,
did not survive.

Lore guztiak usain gabe
geratu dira hementxe;
sasietako orri motza ikusten duzu kolorge,
eta limoiek,
laranja hoiek,
zaporea galdu dute.

Haritza, egun triste hartan,
hola mintzatu zitzaidan.
Libertatea Iortu nuen katea apurtu zenean,
baina bihotza
geldo ta hotza
neukan nire bularrean.
Bihurtu zaitek haranera,
hemen aspertu bazara.
Senda luzea har ezazu, begitu gabe atzera.
Zure gogoa
ezta, gajoa,
itzuliko eremura.

III. Sedan eginiko gogoeta eroak

Animalia ederra,
gizon akabatua.
Lurreko jabe laztana,
zeruek maitatua.
Jaungoiko poteretsuak,
eskuz bedeinkatua.

Ezneunkan izenik ere,
mendietatik zeihar.
Erantzun egunari,
egiten dugu negar.
Herririk herrik genbiltzan,
tristuraz eta makal.

Gatazka hamorratua,
burrukaldi hertsia.
Buztina hilaren kontra,
genbiltzan izakiak.

All the flowers
lost their fragrance;
the brambles . . . stumpy and lackluster,
the lemons,
and those oranges,
taste of nothing.

That sad day the oak tree
spoke thus to me.
I was freed when my chain was broken,
but my heart
was cold and still
in my chest cavity . . .
Return to the valley
if you're tired of this.
Take the long road, don't look back.
your tormented spirit
won't ever return
to this wasteland.

III. Stupid thoughts along the way

Gorgeous animal,
done man.
Darling master of the earth,
beloved of heaven.
Blessed by the hand
of a powerful god.

I didn't even have a name
in my time on the mountains.
We answered to each day,
and cried along the way.
We traveled villages,
saddened, spent.

It was a battle to the death,
in close combat, with weapons.
Living creatures
against dead clay,

Ilunpeko erreinutik,
agertu zen bizia.

Amak amoriotsuak,
aitak bihotz-gogorrak.
Gurasoek elkarrekin,
bake ondoko gerrak.
Alimentatzen dituzte,
derrigorrean haurrak.

Gizona ihes egiteko,
katigatasunetik.
Erdi bitan partizen da,
guztiz engañaturik.
Gorputza eta arima,
erratuz dabil beti.

Ingude-mailu artean,
hauzirik zaharrena.
Eztira konforme izanen
andrea ta gizona.
Burnia trabailatzeko,
behar da lan zekena.

IV. Lizardia

Orain eznago hor, eremu latz horretan;
eznaiz itzuliko egundo sekuletan
abandonatu dudan harizti beltzera.
Senda erpinetik hartu nuen bidea;
sentitu nuen han lepoan ingudea,
baina eznuen bihurtu bururik atzera.

Arbola batetik esan zidan beleak:
zar egin duk horrek, zutik den abereak,
nire anaia maite arranoarekin?
Harrixka batetik, damu haundiarekin,
bareak ziostan: Anai sugearekin,
pisti basati horrek, zer duk horrek egin?

until from the kingdom of darkness
life emerged.

To escape captivity
man
splits in two,
the fool.
Body and soul,
as if that were true.

Anvil and hammer
keep the oldest dispute.
Men and women
never can agree.
Ironsmithery is as hard
as hard can be.

IV. The Ashwood

I'm no longer there, in that wasteland;
I will never return, never ever,
to the black Oakwood I left behind.
I took the steep downward path,
feeling the heavy anvil on my neck
and, yet, not once did I turn back.

From a treetop a crow spoke to me:
tell me upright biped, what did you do
with my bird sister, the eagle?
And from a rock, sliding very slow,
the slug moaned: and with snake brother,
you wild beast, what did you do?

Makila batekin beleari kolpea
eman nion, eta heriotze dorpea
errezibitu zuen niganeik txoriak.
Handik berehala zapaldu ere nuen
nire abarrekin barea, eta eznituen
behatzetan sentitu adur itsusiak.

Astiro nenbilen lizardi zaharrean,
haltura haundiko arbola baten pean,
trankil jezarri nintzen, atseden hartzera.
Giza-itxurako zimu batzuk, haunidak,
ikusi nituen, eta beren geziak
jaurtikitzen zitutzen zeruaren kontra,.

Aldarri batzukin dantza bat egin zuten.
Zeru goibeletik trumoia zen entzuten;
haren oihartzunean ikusi ninduten.
Halaz ikaratu ziren denak biziro;
haien artetik bat etorri zen astiro,
eta nire aurrean belaunikatu zen.

Gizon edo andre, harnasa edo gogoa,
mintzatu zitzaidan zimuaren ahoa,
begiak altzatzera ausartu gaberik.
Goitik hasarreak honera ekarri zaitu,
zeruko bularra gustik zauritu baitu
gure sineskeriak, itsu gaudelarik.

Zimua bazara orduan ni gizona,
baina hau bazara, ni naiz jaungoiko ona,
esan nuen tristerik nire kolkorako.
Zutik jarri zaitek, egizu faborea;
orain esaidazu zergatik hau jentea
egun eder honetan dabilen hain txarto.

Nire hitzarekin erorten zen euria,
adarren artean ere oinasturia:
Ekaitz hamorratua zoan edonundik.
Eta zimist batek piztu zuen laharra;
urek amatatu zioten bere garra.
Eguerdian dena zegoen ilunik.

I hit the crow with a stick,
I killed dead the damned bird
so it wouldn't again dare speak.
A similar fate followed the slimy slug
I crushed its blobby body with my foot
and felt nothing, heard not a hoot.

I walked slowly through the old ashwood,
walked until I found a very tall tree
underneath which I sat and slept a bit.
I saw these enormous humanoid chimps
shooting endless arrows
against the wrongness of the sky.

They danced to a series of screams.
The rumble of thunder filled the darkened sky,
lightening revealed me . . .
and they were filled with fear;
one walked forward slowly,
and before me, sank to his knees.

Man or woman, breath or spirit,
thus spoke the chimp,
not daring look at me.
Did an angry god send you
because heaven's heart is broken
through our blind disbelief?

If you're chimp then I'm man,
but if you're man then I'm god,
I said sadly to myself.
Stand up, please, and tell me
why are your people so sad
on a day as beautiful as this.

Rain fell as he spoke,
thunder hit the trees,
the furious storm zigzagged
and lightning burst a bush on fire,
but rain tamed the flames
and by midday all was darkness

Ilunpean loak ninduen guztiz hartu;
biharamua arte eznintzen jada itzartu:
Hamiltegui batean aparte egon nintzen.
Egun berriaren argiaren heltzean,
animali batzuk zeuden nire aurrean,
jainkoari bitina eskeiniak ziren.

Nire bekokian etzegoen izotza.
Teilatu batean erramu ta ereinotza,
nire gorputz gainean, zeuden hadatuak.
Auspez belauniko, letariak kantatuz,
egunsentiari intzentsua botatuz,
zimuek ziruditen abere mutuak.

Jaungoiko bortitza, guztirik haltuena,
mintzatu zintzaidan zimurik ederrena,
zure apaiz nausia izendatu naute.
Basoan gauean hartu dugun ihiza,
zuri zor dizugun ohore baten gisa,
otoi, har zazu, arren, deus ukatu gabe.

Hemen dadukazu basurde izugarria,
beraren ondoan orein maitagarria,
erbia, galeperra, azerri maltzurra.
Zuhaitzetik ere hartu dugu frutua:
Mertxica gozoa, laranja doratua,
sagarra, madaria, masusta ta intzaurra.

Eskuetan nuen hartu nire makila,
erakutsi nien mehatxuz ukabila,
ahotik hitz zakarrak zitzaizkidan irten.
Espanturekin zimutxo lotsatiak,
otsoaren larruz zebiltzan basatiak,
alde guztietatik eskapatu ziren.

Gorputz eta frutak
pilatu nituen.
Ospel legorrez
fobera haundi
bat nien
irakezi,

I fell into the thickest sleep,
didn't wake until day,
alone in an abyss,
and as the new light rose
I discerned animals around me,
sacrificial offerings to a god.

No frost adorned my forehead
but plaited laurel branches
crowned my head.
Singing litanies, eyes on the ground,
lost, on their knees, the beasts
rose their incense to the sun.

God Almighty, all-powerful,
said the handsomest chimp,
has designated me high priest.
Tonight's hunt is our offering,
our debt to your honor,
please accept it, please.

Here is the gorgeous boar
and here the sweet deer
here the hare, the quail, the clever fox,
from the trees we've taken fruits
the tasty apricot, the golden orange,
the apple, the pear, berries, walnuts.

I brandished my stick,
and threatened with my fist,
I shouted harsh words of displeasure;
the shy little chimps,
wild creatures in wolf skins
scattered, running from me.

Bodies and fruits
I piled;
I gathered wood,
made a bonfire,
destroyed
their sordid

tributu ziki
guztiak erre
zitezen.
Gorpuz eta frutak
pilatu nituen.

Gauzok ikusten diren
lizari dollorra!
munduan zerbait
bada zu zara
zaharra!
Nire lepoan
jarri zenidan
uztarriaren
Gauzok ikusten diren
lizardi dollora!

Nire begi berdeak
eztira orain itsu.
Suak arinki
eskeintzak erre
baititu
bere kean
nire gogoa
osorik nuen
garbitu.
Nire begi berdeak
eztira orain itsu!

Nik hartu nion osotoro
lizardi hari gorroto.
Zuzi batekin erre nuen arboladia dongero:
gizonak eztu
erraz arteztu
bidegaberik egundo.

Zimultatea su-garretan
zen kiskailduko benetan;
Beren hogenak pagatzeko honako mundu honetan,
okasiorik
edo ziorik,
nik eznien batere eman.

offerings.
Bodies and fruits
I piled.

Why have me witness this,
evil ashwood!
If ever there was
something rotten
in the world,
you are it!
You've placed
a heavy yoke
around my neck.
Why have me witness this,
evil ashwood!

My green eyes
are not yet blind.
This fire
quickly burned
the pyre
of offerings,
and its smoke
purified my spirit.
My green eyes
are not yet blind!

I hated the ashwood
with all my heart
and set the forest on fire with glee.
It was never easy
for man to put injustice
right.

I have no doubt
that the chimp family died
and atoned for their sins in this life.
They never had a chance
to explain their side.

Nire atzean nenkusan nik
errauts mehea bakarrik:
Hondamendia, bakarte nardagarria, basorik
deseginena,
hondatuena,
agertzen zen edonundik.

Eta zeruen distizari
zauri gordin bat agiri . . .
Ene bihotza taupadaka ezpainetatik ihesi . . .
Nire odola
zoakon nola
ungentu bat zeruari.

Zapaldu nuen lur tristea
datza ondikoz betea.
Nire zapatok darabilte heriotzeko zortea:
daukate oro,
zuhur ta zoro,
hondatzeko birtutea.

Nire aurrean agertu zat
estrata haltu mehar bat.
Darrigorrean hartuko dut estrata hori bidetzat,
patu oneko
garaiz heltzeko
behar nauen haranerat.

Eta buztinak, egunero,
galdetzen zidan argiro:
zergatik doa beherantza ibiltaria aguro;
guztiz tristerik,
bizi gaberik,
uzten duzu dena gero.

I left behind me
the finest ash;
nothing else, but loneliness, ruin,
and the forest undone,
sterile,
like no other in the world.

A tear of light
broke the sky . . .
My heart galloped right out of my lips . . .
my blood
was a balm
for the spirits.

The sad earth I walk
spreads across
disconsolate,
my feet stomp death's same ground:
all of us
the sane and the fools
fall alike.

Ahead of me I see
a narrow, difficult path.
I know for sure I shall take that one,
to arrive in time
in the valley
where my fate awaits.

And the mud every day
asks
why the walker must head downward
so fast,
so sad,
having left everything behind.

V. Estratan eginiko gogoeta eroak

Goiko basoan elurra,
zuria da ta motza.
Errekaldean zimaurra,
zikina bainan ona.
Gizona zutik munduan,
sugerik zakarrena.

Harrotasunez beterik,
ezkenkien zer egin.
Animaliak tragatu,
halare gizonak hil.
Izenez aldatzen gara,
haizeaz putziturik.

Muntantzak begiratzeko,
ezta asmatu denpora.
Zerren uraren erditik,
agertu zen buztina.
Haizearen deseotik,
agertu ziren urak.

Gure soldadoek gerran,
soinean harmadura.
eskallera luzetatik,
igonik gaztelurra.
Eskuetan espata bat,
hiltzeko zaldun hura.

Dontzellarik ezta aurkitzen,
gizonen joranetan.
Oitura zaharra izan zen,
leen artaxuketa.
Nobioak elkarrekin,
egoteko gauetan.

Babilonian katigu
baikeunden euskaldunak.
Idiak uztarri-pean,

V. Foolish thoughts along the road

Snow in the forest uphill
is ugly and white.
By the river, manure:
a dirty nurture.
Man stands in the world,
wisest among the snakes.

Full of pride,
we know not what to do.
We gulp animals down,
kill men regardless,
change our names,
puff ourselves up with air.

It's not clear at all
when things mutate.
Why in with water
mud appeared.
Why through the wind's desire
water appeared.

Our soldiers arm heavily
for war,
climb long ladders
up castle walls.
Sword in one hand,
ready to kill a knight.

Thanks to man's wishes
all damsels are gone.
There was an old tradition,
to keep nightwatch on the corn,
so boyfriend and girlfriend
got some time alone.

We Basques were
captives in Babylon,
oxen under the yoke,

ziren gure pareak.
Hantxe genbiltzen gu nola,
astoak zama-pean.

Lurpeku eremuetan,
sorginen biltzarrea.
Zeru gaineko aireetan,
jainkoen hasarrea.
Itsasoko hareatzan,
deabruen barrea.

VI. Iratze ederra

Estrata hertsiak ekarri nau honera
liluragarria etzen nire egoera
zezen azkarrak zeuden iratze ederrean.
Bidean eznuen eguzkirik ikusi;
nire esku zikinok eznituen ikusi
iherri igaro nuen hibai gardenean,

Nire odol beroa zerua igon zenean
ugari zitzaidan geratu bularrean:
burutik oinetara zitaldu ninduen.
Arima nendukan elurraren parean;
iherri baino lehen nire gorputz tristea
zimaurteguia bezain zikina zegoen.

Ardien artean agertu zen artzainaxul;
zaldiaren zeian zetorren behor-zaina,
esaten zitadela: etoia, doilorra:
hil duzu gizon bat, eta haren odola
oraindik daukazu esku bietan. Nola
pegatuko diozu orani zure zorra?

Zerri-zainek ere irain egin zidaten;
unaiak zebiltzan arneguak esaten:
Nundik etorri zara, haragi-jalea?
Madarikatua izan zaitek betiko!
Halako lehoirik inun ezta ikusiko,
dezagun hil oraintxe odol-edalea!

that was our role.
And like donkeys
we just
carried the load.

In the realms below
witches gathered.
In the skies above,
gods thundered.
And on the sea's sandy shores,
the devil cackled.

VI – Beautiful fernery

The narrow path brought me here,
I am dazzled by this place.
Playful bulls trot along this fernery,
without sunlight on the way
I never noticed my soiled hands
as I swam across the crystalline stream.

My warm blood reached heaven,
it flowed freely from my chest
and soaked me entirely.
My soul was white as snow;
and my body, before the swim,
as filthy as filth can be.

The shepherd turned up with his sheep,
the muleteer rode in with his horse,
and they beckoned: come you fool!
You have killed a man, and his blood
still stains your hands. How will you
find forgiveness for your soul?

Pig keepers scolded me
cowherds shouted all around:
where did you come from, carnivore?
Damn you for all eternity!
You beast, we never saw the like,
bloodsucker, you must die!

Gizonen eskuak eztu hartzen jainkorik:
lurraren gainean egintza ezinagorik
gure pentsamentuan ezta bururatu.
Iraen artean gantzu batekin nintzen
eskutatu laster, eta arratseko ihintzen
freskura polietan nintzen desgorputzu.

Eskuan gañibet, akuilu ta haizkora,
hiltzeko asmoekin zetorzkidan albora,
baina etzuten aurkitu gorputz hila baizik.
Nire arima berriz, lorez lore kantari,
barre egiten zion jentatze gaiztoari,
ezpaizuten gorputza kausitu bizirik.

Demonio batek sartu dio buruan,
mintzatzen geratu ziren gure inguruan,
harnasa bat bezala, infernuko gatza.
Dagoen lekuan utzi dezagun, eta
hemendik eskapa gaitezen, pozoin eta
maldizio hoiekin ezkaitezen kutsa.

Erori zen gaua abereen gainean,
izotza berekin ekarririk soinean:
Espiritu guztien bildurgarria zen.
Nire arima ere animalietatik
sartu zen, biluzik ez egoteagatik;
gauerdiko jeleri ihes egin zien.

Bildots mantsoari egin nion bisita.
Hartu nuen gero ardi galant polita.
Ahuntzaren esnea nuen pozoatu.
Hutsitu nituen aharien adarrak.
Ebaki nizkion akerrari bizarrak.
Abetxeak nituen osorik larritu.

Behorra zegoen, zaldiaren parean,
ahalke gaberik, astoaren aurrean,
ema —galdu bat— balitz, leket lizunetan,
Buztanetik nion tiratu zaldiari;
irain itsusi bat niotsan mandoari:
Sakon sartu nintzaien aaide-kontuetan.

The hands of men cannot touch God;
it cannot happen on the earth, we know,
it isn't an entertainable thought,
so I hid deep among the ferns,
soothed my skin with a balm
and disembodied in the cool evening air.

They came with knives, spears and axes,
ready, intent on killing me,
but all they found was a lifeless body;
my soul leaped through the blooms
laughing at the miserable fools
who saw nothing there but a husk.

He had a devil inside,
I heard them say by my side,
a soul that sprung from hell.
Let us leave things as they are,
let's escape this place and all contact,
everything here is poisoned and damned.

Night spread its blanket over the cattle
the fields dressed up in frost:
all around the spirits shook,
my soul passed through the beasts
to shield its nakedness; their warmth
a shelter from the cold night air.

I stood next to the docile lamb
and embraced a gorgeous ewe.
I poisoned the goat's milk,
from the ram I took his horns,
and clipped the beard of the billy goat.
All to sow discord in the stables.

A horse mounted a mare lustfully,
next to the donkey; clearly,
they enjoyed the obscenity.
I pulled the horse's tail;
insulted the gormless ass,
I had much to say about their family affairs.

Heldu nintzen gero zerrien gorputzera,
eta kendu nion apoari makera;
haragi sendoalak argaldu nizkien.
Buzkantza, lupua, odoleste gozoa,
urdaiazpiroa, urdaia, solomoa,
zizarearen gisen, guztia jan nien.

Katuari nion jan-arazi zimaurra;
bisigu-zalea bihurtu zen zakurra:
adiskidetu ziren amodio onarekin.
Oiloek zioten oilarrari kolpatu;
oila-lokak ere arraultzetan pikatu.
Ahateek hegoira zuten ihes egin.

Gau luze bateko bidaje latzgarriak
barkatu zizkidan nire kulpa guztiak,
lixiba berri batez garbitu bainintzen.
Nire babesetik atera nintzenean,
egun berri hartan, hiltamu latz batean,
animali guztiak akabatu ziren.

Laster sentutu nuen
egunaren hotza.
nire ahoan
zapore siku
mingotsa.

Iratz artean
bilatu nuen
arinki nire
gorputza.
Laster sentitu nuen
egunaren hotza.

Eztut igarten nola
nagoen bizirik.
Aurrerantzean
eztut izango
lotsarik.

Soon after I reached the pigsty
and took the sow from the swine,
their flesh I left bloodless, clean,
hung the intestines and ate
the ham, the loins, the belly,
the sausages, the bacon, I ate fully.

I gave the cat the leftovers,
and to my dog a delicate fish,
and they bonded over this,
while the hens fought the cocks,
destroyed the eggs they hatched,
and ducks flew far, far south.

That treacherous journey of the night
atoned for all the sins that I had;
I had been bleached bright white.
When I came out of my refuge
in the new day's light, the animals,
after a long agony, all died.

Soon I felt
the cool early air
and in my mouth
a taste of
something dry, and bitter.

Among the ferns
my body
was still there
soon I felt
the cool early air.

I don't quite understand
why I'm still alive
but from now on
I won't
feel shame.

Ezpailegoke
nire arima
gau hontan bezain
biluzik.
Eztut igarten nola
nagoen bizirik.

Bildur haundiagorik
eztut erakutsi.
Nire gorputzaz
nintzen poliki
ni jantzi;
eztut eginen
nire arima
azergatikan
erantzi.
Bildur haundiagorik
eztut erakutsi.

Eta gizonek zerdukaten
bidegabeok zer ziren;
gizonen berri zorrotzean sekula ere ezpaitzen
hangoa bezain
heriotz bezain
itsusirik presentatzen.

Gurekin dabil deabrua,
sutan baitoa zerua.
Arima gaizto etoi batek irauli digu dornua.
Ezin geiago,
egun baitago
lur gainean infernua.

Deabruentzat bakarrik da
heriotze bat, polita:
bilo guztiak tiratuka sustrai beretik kenduta,
lepotik hartu,
ahoan sartu
urregorrizko taketa.

My soul can never again
be the way it was that night,
I don't quite understand
why I'm still alive.

I never
showed fear.
I put my body on
again
slowly.
I will never
ever again
unleash
my soul.
I never
showed fear.

Men: what's wrong with them,
they can never find their way,
straight and narrow they don't comprehend,
nothing uglier
than all that death
has ever manifested.

The devil is with us
because fires burn in heaven;
he stirs our most treacherous souls
and nothing can be done,
because hell is with us
now, here, on this very soil.

For the devil
only one death will do:
pull his hair from its root,
grab his neck,
and stuff in his mouth
a golden stake.

Deabru beltza hil dezagun!
egon gaitezen fededun! -—
zioten, eta haien esanak entzuten ziren edonun.
—Gizon ortutsa;
haren gorputza:
arin erre dezaiogun!

Handik joan ziren iratzera,
nire gorputza hartzera.
Kantu ederrak ezpainetik, otoitz luzeak zerura,
poliki zoan
bide gaiztoan
gizaldea ni hiltzera.

Hara allegatu zirenean
bildurtu ziren benetan.
Nire gorputza etzegoen paratu nuen lekuan;
espantu latza,
izu garratza,
zedukaten ezpainetan.

Ni banindoan kantaturik
galtzada legun batetik.
Zer egin nuen eznenkien, eztut jakin nai ezer nik:
Nire gauzetan,
azioetan
eztago zuzenbiderik.

VII. Galtzadan eginiko gogoeta eroak

Zer garen guk eztakigu,
inoiz ezta jakingo.
Anketan oinak ditugu,
lurretik ibilteko.
Besoetan esku finak,
gauzak erabilteko.

Gizonak eztu pausurik,
hil eztadin artean.

Let us kill the devil
let us stay in the faith,
their shouts rang all around.
Let us now burn
the body
of the barefoot man.

They went to the fernery
in search of my body,
they sang beautifully, they prayed to heaven,
they walked leisurely
as they moved
to destroy me.

When they arrived
they felt really afraid,
my body was not where I'd laid,
horror twisted their faces,
their lips curled in fear,
terror filled the air.

And I walked away singing
down the pretty road
oblivious to everything.
I didn't want to know
the things that I did,
my actions
escape all reasoning.

VII – Inane thoughts along the road

We don't know what we are,
and we shall never know.
Our legs have feet,
and thus we walk the earth.
Our arms have dexterous hands,
and thus we use and make things.

Man can never stop
until the moment of his death.

Hil bere iloba maitea,
egin du amandreak.
Ezta eguzkirik agertu,
egun bodei-artean.

Modu asko daude hemen,
odolak edateko.
Ezpainarekin edo-ta,
ezpata bitarteko.
Bidea bilatu dute,
guri gaztigazteko.
Hibai ondoko landetan,
belar gizena dago.
Haurrok dugu gogoreko,
askozaz nahiago.
Borobiltasun emea,
zorroztasuna baino.

Neskatxa garbiak dira,
hemendik desagertu.
Ezta dontzelleziarik,
inundik ere urratu.
Zerren alu-lore gabe,
neskak dirade sortu.

Erdaldunen ingudean,
probatu zen indarra.
Harriarekin entramak,
galduko ditu zerrak.
Atzo deserritu dugu
esposa bat izorra.

Lamiak arrekaldean
urrezko orrazia
Madarikatu izan bedi,
zerorren askazia.
Ematen espadidazu
amaren artasia.

A grandmother may kill
her favorite grandkid.
The sun may never
come through the clouds.

Many are the ways
to drink blood.
Maybe through the lips,
sometimes through the sword.
They'd find a way
to punish us anyway.
The shores of the river
are lush with fat grass.
It's much better
to think of the children instead.
Much preferable their innocence
to the bluntness of this life.

Pure girls
no longer exist,
virginity
is not lost anymore.
Girls come deflowered
into the world.

We tested our strength
on foreign anvil.
The sierra
swallowed its sharp peaks.
Yesterday we banished
a pregnant lady.

The river nymphs,
the golden comb.*
Damned be
your freedom,
unless you give me now
your mother's scissors.

VIII. Lore-mendia

Orain hemen nago, lore-mendi honetan.
Nire gogoetak eginik, gailurretan
armenda loratuen parea naiz orain.
Orain eznago han, lurralde hotz haietan.
Misterio guztiak ulerturik benetan,
nire arima eztago mirari baten zain.

Bidean hartu dut menturazko harnasa.
Eztaukat lehengo dudetako metaza,
askaturik baitago korapilotxo hau.
Hodei eta errainu guztiak urraturik,
sentitzen ezpaita inun sufrimenturik,
galtzada legun batek honera ekarri nau.

Arrosa politak, krabelina-liliak,
orkideak eta gardeni-begoniak,
baratz honetan daude mila lore eder.
Nire sudurra da osorik liluratu.
Etzait zentzu hori orain arte guztatu:
Orain horrez gainera eztakit nik ezer.

Usainetan dator nireganantz bizia.
Landare-gogoak estaldurik guztia,
arimako zizare guztiak hil dira.
Intzentsu berrion arima zait usandu;
Uhin urrintsuok usteltasuna jan du:
Ederki di biziak ematen begira.

Pausa-leku hori nuen atzo hautatu,
gorputza ta arima egkeko mainatu,
ezlezaten eduki orbantxo batere.
Ungentuetarik hartu nuen gantzua,
arrats freskoari bota nion zantzua:
eznaiz egon inoiz bart bezain alegere.

Baratz honetara atzo nintzen etorri.
Kolore guztiak, beilegi, more, gorri,
lilietan zaizkigu agertzen hemendik.

VIII. Flower mountain

Now I'm here, in this flower mountain,
lost in thought, on the peaks,
and, like an almond tree, I bloom.
I'm no longer in cold landscapes.
I have come to understand all mysteries
and my soul expects no miracles.

On the road I breathed my fate
lost the yarn of doubt,
freed up its little knot.
Tearing up every cloud,
I left no room for suffering,
and walked up this lovely road.

Beautiful roses, lilies, carnations,
orchids, gardenias and begonias,
a thousand flowers in this field of dreams,
my nose, my sense, never inhaled
anything as heavenly and exquisite:
I never want anything else, this is it.

Life reaches me in smells.
The essence of flowers in everything
killed every parasite in my soul.
Incense perfumed my entire being,
its fragrance destroyed all rottenness.
Life looks at me again with limpid eyes.

Yesterday I chose that restful place,
to care for body and soul,
and disguise every little scar.
I found a good balm that I applied,
and shouted into the cool night.
Last night was my happiest.

I arrived yesterday in this field.
The lilies come in every color,
Yellow, purple, red; all there.

Eta baratzainak izena dauka Miren:
bere begietan lore guztiak ziren;
dontzella da garbia, engañu gaberik.

Galtzada zelaitik nekaturrik nentorren.
Ahatzirik neunkan iratze berde horren
hildoetan pairatu nuen pasioa.
Odolezko izerdi gorria isuri nuen;
pañolo batekin negar-tantak nituen
legortu: Urte beteko arnegazioa . . .

Amaitu zenean galtzada luze hori,
zentzu gabe nintzen kir gainean erori,
arrosadi bateko aihenaren kontra.
Neskatila honen besartean esnatu
nintzen, zidalako baltzeo bat kantatu,
egungo oilaritean, txorien gisara.

Miren eder hori zen nire baltsamoa:
esku legunekin ukiturik ahoa,
zer den bake narea erakutsi zidan.
Seinale bakan bat eginez sudurrean,
oroitu zitzaidan hil zena gurutzean,
predikaru zuena mundutik atean.

Bere besartean baratz zogarria:
ugatzak arrosaz, krabelinaz gorria;
arreba nausi baten nengoen altzoan.
Lore-mendia zen bere gorputz bikaina.
Nire gorputzean sartu zen baratzaina:
Eskerronez ninduen hornitu ariman.

Zekiat nor haizen eta nundik hatorren,
zekiat zer haizen, honera zerk hakarren:
Nire laguntasuna eskeintzen dauat nik.
Kontuz ibilteko diotsat anaiari,
iguriki nion ene maitaleari:
eztrauat edireten gainean kulparik.

Hemen ere entzun duk, zabal, bire berria,
hitzak esan duten gauza tamalgarria;

The gardener's name is Miren:
Every flower blooms in her eyes,
she's pure, she has nothing to hide.

I walked easily down the road.
Left in the green ferns behind
my sorrows buried in furrows.
My sweat was blood red,
and I dried it with a handkerchief:
it soaked up one year of pain.

When I came to the end of the road,
I fainted and fell on the soil,
crashing against a rose bush.
I woke in the arms of a girl
who sang a waltz like a bird,
with dawn, she sang to me.

She, the gorgeous Miren, was my balm:
her soft fingers touched my lips
and taught me what peace means.
With a single gesture above my nose,
she reminded me of he who died on the cross,
and preached from the threshold of the world.

Her embrace was a wondrous garden:
roses her breasts; her waist, carnations;
I felt safe in my big sister's arms.
Her beautiful body was a flower mountain;
she was the gardener of my life,
through her, my soul was soothed.

I know who you are and where you come from,
I know what you are, and what brought you here:
I am here to help you, that's my offering,
I tell you brother be careful, avoid
meeting my lover along the way,
although I know you're not to blame.

I've heard what they say about you
the terrible things they say you did;

laborariak zeudek hi katigatu nai:
Jarriko drauate lepoan uztarria,
katea batekin, lotuko zaik garria:
eginen haute gero mandoaren anai.

Hire aurrean duk zabaldu kaminoa;
eztuk ogia jan, eztuk edan arnoa,
bazekiat haizela egarri ta gose.
Mila legoako kamino hau, luzea,
ibili behar duk orain, ene maitea,
arinki, galdu gabe denpora batere.

Lore-mendi maitea
milikatu nuen.
Ezpainak hango
arrosan jarri
nituen.
Ederkien ikasi nuen
usain gozoak
dastatzen.
Lore-mendi maitea
milikatu nuen.

Baratz laztangarria
harturik eskuan,
nire hegalak
hedaturikan
airean,
beste gabe
paratu nintzen
herrietara
bidean
baratz laztangarria
harturik eskuan.

Arriskuen aurrean
eznaiz bildurtia:
apaindu nuen
hegaldatzeko
gurdia;
urrinetan

the farmhands want to punish you,
bind your neck with a heavy yoke;
make you walk the donkey.

The road opens ahead of you;
you ate no bread, drank no wine,
I know you thirst and hunger.
This path of the thousand leagues
you must walk for now, my love;
hurry now, hurry you must leave.

I tasted the honey
of my beloved flower mountain.
I kissed
the rose
on its peak.
How well I learned
to savor the taste
of its subtle scent.
I tasted the honey
of my beloved flower mountain.

Held by the hand
of my garden refuge
I spread
my wings to the wind,
and without pause
walked on
to the villages.
Held by the hand
of my garden refuge.

I'm not afraid,
I can face risks,
I set my cart
ready
for flight.
I took a deep breath

nintzen orduan
dupin-arteko
hordia.
Arriskuen aurrean
eznaiz bildurtia.

Solo artean landareak
galdu zituen loreak.
Aiher ziren bihotzetikan etsai etoiak, nireak.
Leku haietan,
ortu dehetan,
soilik zeuden laboreak.
Ordu bateko letariak
esan zizkidan gariak:
Hoek dira landare motzek darabilzkiten sariak.
Eztut esango
direla hango
umetxoak martiriak.

Artadi luze legortuak
zarratu dizkit portuak
horrenbeste indarrik eztu egin sekula artoak.
Neska-sorgina,
oi-erregina,
ernatu zuen ortuak.

Benetan dela ausardia,
benetan dela garbia,
polit, galant eta dotore, gorotz artsan arbia:
bere arreba,
bere izeba,
izorra den ahardia.

Egiazki da iraunkorra
moztu gabeko ilarra.
Badirudi hortz-egin gabe enia-galdu bat, zaharra.
Neska pottola
badabil nola
aingeru bat zerutarra.

and let the scent
go to my head.
I'm not afraid
I can face risks.

On the patch all plants
had lost the blooms.
How I hate the enemies of my heart,
right here in this land,
on every field,
all the men who only toil.
In its time of litanies
wheat wanted to sing a song,
that's how a humble plant finds joy.
You won't hear me say
poor children today
are martyrs.

A long dry cornfield
closes in on me,
never before has corn pushed so hard.
The crops bloomed and bloomed
for the girl-witch
for the good queen.

It truly is daring,
it truly is clean,
beautiful, handsome, and neat,
the turnip sitting on the dung heap:
its sister,
its aunt,
the pregnant sow.

It's permanent it's true
in the branch the pea is stuck.
Looks like an old toothless whore.
And the girl so plump
jolly as anything
walks like a heavenly angel.

Haundiegia hamorrua
hartu zuena porrua.
Nagel gorriz, orin beilegiz, zikindu zaio txirula.
Orraztu ditu
eta garbitu
bere biloen kirrua.
Konorte gabe dagoela
bere ortuan kipula.
Soinu gabe mutiko-dantzan entzun diogu txirula.
Bart arratsean,
bart iluntzean,
agatu zuen kaiola.

IX. Kaminoan eginiko gogoeta eroak

Demonioen artean
politena Belial.
Begi politak ditugu,
galantak aurpegian.
Mundua konprenitzeko
ezkara animaliek.
Gauza haundiak egiten
ditugu lur gainean.
Eztago pizti batere,
inungo lurraldean.
Pentsatuko eztuena,
ezkarena erregeak.

Gizona atinik lurrean,
komunari begira.
Satza jateko gogoak,
molde askotako dira.
Gorotzak eta gernuak
eman dute begira.

Josepe arotza zen beti,
gizon guztiz prestua.
Senideek ta hauzoek,
franko estimatua.

The leek lost it
far and above it.
Its flute was a mess; now yellow, now red.
It combed,
it washed its beard.
Meanwhile in the patch
the onion got dizzy
and collapsed.
We heard a mute flute
play the boy dance, mutiko-dantza.
Yesterday evening
late at night,
the jail stood empty and dark.

IX. Crazy thoughts along the road

Among all demons
the handsomest is Belial;
our eyes the prettiest
on that face, so special.
We are no animals,
not made to understand the world.
We do great things
on this earth.
And there isn't a beast
I bet
who won't agree
we are kings.

Man lies on the ground,
observing the latrines.
The desire to eat waste
can go either way,
here now is the piss,
over there now, the shit.

The carpenter Joseph
was known to be a good man.
Relatives and neighbors
held him in great esteem,

Bere egitate denetan
egoten zen sentzua.

Ema-galduak debiltza
lixibatan sartuta.
Esklaba haren gorputza,
merkatuan salduta.
Eta bere arima aratza,
zerurako galduta.

Zerutik bart erori zen
harri bat borobila.
Zeruen urdintasuna
harriz dago egina.
Jainkoen usteltasun
dugu ostrailikia.

Gorbeia baino gorago
askozaz goragoa.
Arginek egin digute
harmore bat haltua.
Izena jerri diote,
apaizek itsasoa.

X. Herri-bitartea

Eskutatu ginen gaztelu gaitz batean.
Maitaleak ziten eztan ohe berean,
baina guk ezkenuen bekaturik egin.
Gure oeriztea eztator haragkik;
larruko orduetan ezta gauza politik.
Bakarrik nai genuen egon elkarrekin.

Herri-bitarteko alkate nagusia
etorri zitzaigun; senideen hauzia
ekarririk: Baneunkan judizio berria.
Berekin zetortzan: arotza, igeltserua,
zapataria ta baita erlojerua,
lege-gizona eta errementaria.

everything he did
was always right.

Whores soak up
in bleach.
A slave girl sits
in the market square,
waiting for her soul
to be denied paradise.

Yesterday a round stone
fell from heaven.
The blue of the skies
is made of rocks,
and that rainbow
is the poop of the gods.

Beyond Mount Gorbea,
much, much higher above,
bricklayers built
a high wall made of stones.
And priests, as they do,
have named it
the sea: *itxaso*.

X. Crosstowns

We came to hide in a big castle,
and as lovers lay on the same bed
but we didn't sin all the same,
because our passion was not of the flesh;
there is beauty beyond the fusion of bodies,
and we sought an alternate kind of union.

The mayor of Crosstowns
found us; along with him came
the elders: they'll judge us, I thought.
He brought the carpenter, the bricklayer,
the shoemaker, the watchmaker,
the ironsmith, and to top it all, the lawyer.

Bakoitza jezarri zen kadira batean:
lege-gizona ta alkatea ezkerrean,
apaiza, dendaria, berriz, eskumatik.
Esan ni.en: «Jaunak! Abere-tratuetan:
ez naiz markataria, eztut eroaten nik.

Agure biltzarrak mendatari, honera
bidaldu grauzkitzu, zerorri galdetzera
Jainkoaren semea egiaz bazara.
Eztut inoiz ere esan borrelakorik,
baina munduetan gizon gertuagorik
kausituko eztuzue, ez joan aurrera.

Apaiza altzatu zen berehala hasarrez.
—Birao egin baitu—, esanik deiadarrez,
—apurtu behar ditut ene soinekoak.
Gero niri esan zidan: —Zeruetako
ateak eztira ideki zuretzako.
Zure ugazabak dira jaungoiko faltsoak.

Errege bazara, edo Jaungoikoa;
zure predikua mundu honetakoa
ezpada, orain bertontxe esan behar duzu
zure poterak, gizon-gainditasunak,
eman nork zizkitzun. Eta nire erantzunak
gutxi tardatu zuen: ez nik, zuk diozu.

Gero altzatu zen lege-gizon maltzurra.
Hortzak irriturik, egin zidan agurra,
sakon sartu zidena barnean ziria.
— Eztago jainkorik legearen aurrean,
eta gizon batek egiten duenean
hogenik haundiena ezta miraria.

—Preso omendau gaztelu gaitz honetan,
dorre meharrean, dontzella guztietan
hoberena, ederrena, neska garbiena.
Haren ahideek hauzia dekartsue;
judikatu gabe kondenatu zaitue;
behar duzu iaguntza, aiskide batena.

Each took their rightful seat:
The mayor and the lawyer to the left,
and the priest and the shopkeeper to the right
I told them: Sirs! I know nothing
about the cattle mart, I know not
how to sell or how to buy.

"The council of elders sent us here,
all of us you see,
to check if you may be the son of God."
I never said such a thing,
but I warn you, you've never seen
a man more determined than me.
Stop, don't move an inch!

The priest stood up angrily.
"You blasphemer! How dare you!
I shall rend my garments."
And then addressed me: "the gates
of heaven shall never open for you.
I know you've been sent by false gods."

"If you're a king, or a God,
if your words are not of this world,
tell us right now, I command,
whose superhuman powers these are,
who gave them to you." I answered without hesitation,
what can I do, you say it all: you ask and you respond.

Then the astute lawyer stood up,
and greeted me through gritted teeth,
he dug his eyes deep into me, and said
"there is no God before the law,
and when a man commits a crime
no miracles will save his side."

"They say you locked up in this castle,
in its furthest tower, the fairest damsel
in the realm; the prettiest, the purest.
Her relatives accuse you,
they judge and condemn you
before going to court;
You, my friend, need a friend."

—Etor bitez orain honera lekukoak;
hontaz piedatea euki beza jainkoak.
Preso dagoenaren betorzkigu ilobak.
Zetortzan: Sei ziren, sei aingeru dotore
eta etzidaten eman ezein amore.
Hain antza dohatsurik etzeukan izebak.

—Ohostu zenuen gure izeba maitea.
Egun hauetako baratzaren tristea!
Eztaukagu jadanik norekin jokatu.
Hau egin digunak merezi du hiltzea.
Ezta gauza erreza beroni barkatzea,
osin ilun batean hamildu baikaitu.

Probuak itzazu presenta zure alde.
Perpausa guztia izanen da debalde:
epaia eman gaberik kondenatu zara . . .
—Galdetzen bazaio andregai nireari,
berak esanen du zergatik, hegalari,
ihes egin genuen gaztelu hontara.

—Gurutze batetik zintzilik hil artean
josiko zaitugu biharko goizaldean—
mintzatu zen hbzenki epai-emalea.
Etzaitezen egon bakarrik tormentuan,
beste aldetikan josiko dugu orduan,
burnizko lokarriez zure maitalea.

— Geiegi duk, jauna, ene oneriztea;
bildurgarria duk, ezain heriotzea,
indak indar haundia, ahul duk usoa!
— Aingeru guztien bizitegui erdian,
aitaren aurrean, biharko eguerdian,
izanen naiz betiko zure esposoa.

Gure gorputz argalak
desegindu ziren,
leze batera
astiro jatsi
baikinen.
Bizkarrean

"Now, call your witnesses,
and may God take pity on you.
First we call the lady's young cousins."
They came: six, six heavenly angels,
none of whom would help me.
Not even their auntie looks as beatific.

"Bring proof to your defense,
because everything you say is in vain:
You've been judged without a jury."
If you asked my beloved,
she would tell you here and now
why to this castle we eloped.

"Tomorrow you will hang on the cross,
from dawn until you're no more,"
said the judge hoarse and loud.
"And so you don't suffer such torment alone,
we shall hang your lover by your side,
bound in the heaviest of chains."

"Lord, my love for you is too great,
but still, I'm afraid of death,
I am your weak dove, please give me strength!
Surrounded by legions of angels,
at midday tomorrow, before our Father,
we shall be man and wife forever."

Our thin bodies
disappeared,
slowly
we descended
into the abyss.
We both

gurutze hura
biok eraman
genuen.
Gure gorputz argalak
desegindu ziren.

Arbola artez zuzena,
gurutze pisua.
Beti betiko
izanen zara
gurtua.
Seinalea,

ezaugarria,
oroitarria,
leinua.
Arbola artez zuzena
gurutze pisua.

Imajina bakarra,
santu biribila.
Zeure izenean
eginen dira
eun mila
bidegabe
eta ezpataz
hutsitugo da
magina.
Imajina bakarra,
santu biribila.

Zutirik dago gurutzea;
hurbildu zaigu hiltzea.
Gure oinetan algaraka arinki doa jentea,
gure aurrean
dagoenean
presente heriotzea.

Gaurko goizean borreruak
zabaldu ditu zeruak.
Hauk dira nire suin-erranak, nire erreinuko primuak

carried
that cross
on our backs.
Our thin bodies
disappeared.

Oh upright tree,
oh heavy cross.
Forever
you shall
be adored.
Symbol,
sign,
memory,
lineage.
Oh upright tree,
oh heavy cross.

Eternal image,
holy symbol.
In your name
thousands
of wrongs
have been compelled,
and still
they'll draw
the sword
from the sheath.
Eternal image,
holy symbol.

The cross stands,
death is near.
At our feet
hordes scream,
sensing the closeness
of our final breath.

The executioner this morning
opened the heavens.
"These are my in-laws, my cousins, and they shall inherit the kingdom.

On deritzaiet.
Mandatu haiek
lotu zituzten munduak.

Nire juboia ta alkandora
galtza luzeak ta fraka,
Mirenen gona zetazkoa eta atorra polita:
Ebatsi dube,
oostu digute
gure jantzia barreka.

Apostoluak eztoazi
niregandikan ihesi,
Nik esandako kantikarik inork ezpaitu ikasi
Hainbat amore, ezta sekula ikusi.

Nire bularrak urraturik,
geratu nintzen bakarrik.
Asmo onetako hondamendi hontan eztaukat zergatik
iraun geiago.
Arima dago
gorputza kendu nahirik.

XI. Requiem

Nire arima hegalariak
gozatu baitu zerua,
LURPEAN DATZA EHORTZIRIKAN,
NIRE GORPUTZ USTELDUA.

Orain eztago nire barnean
lehen neunkan hamorrua,
huts-hutsik nago nola binintzen
ijitoen gatilua,
ta karutean diamanteak
saltzen diren merkatua:
LURPEAN DATZA EHORTZIRIKAN,
NIRE GORPUTZ USTELDUA.
Nire hilobi gainean hasi

I wish them well."
His words strangled
the world.

My jacket and my shirt,
my pants, my shoes.
Miren's silk skirt and graceful blouse:
They cut them off,
they stole from us,
and they laughed.

The apostles are here,
they won't ever leave.
No one learned the song I sang.
I never knew
love like this.

Finally I am alone,
with my heart all torn.
There's no more hope in this endeavor,
I can give up now.
My soul is ready
to leave my body.

XI. Requiem

My winged soul
flies happy heavenward,
MY BODY LIES AND ROTS
DOWN IN THE EARTH BELOW.

I no longer feel the fury
that burned deep inside me,
I find myself empty,
like the gypsies' casserole,
like the market where diamonds
sell at prices well beyond.
MY BODY LIES AND ROTS
DOWN IN THE EARTH BELOW.
The thistles on my tombstone

dela kimatzen kardua,
bere sustarrak dit kilikatu
nire belaun zurrundua:
nigana heldu baitzait hozendi
ez-mugitzeko ordua,
LURPEAN DATZA EHORTZIRIKAN,
NIRE GORPUTZ USTELDUA.

Orain eztago nire gorputza
inolare bilutzua;
nire tunika baita oraintxe
maite ninduen mundua,
nire arima ezin legoke
ezergatik lotsatua.
LURPEAN DATZA EHORTZIRIKAN,
NIRE GORPUTZ USTELDUA.

XII. Deskantsuaren bitartez

Etxean bezala gaude
orain arrokartean.
Adiskideak gara
egintza bakoitzean
Joane eta Miren,
altzipresen artean
usteldu garenean
Nola diren luze
altzipresak gausan!
Hilotz ustelek elkar
maitatzen dutenean,
ezta diferentziarik
hezurrutsen artean.

Mila gezur esan zigun
atzo gure maisuak;
gizon hilak ezkara
gizon eskolatuak:
Ikusten ditugu
beraren liburuak,
nola abere mutuak

have started to bloom,
and a root tickles my knee,
time has come
for me to remain still.
MY BODY LIES AND ROTS
DOWN IN THE EARTH BELOW.

It is not true to say
that my body is naked;
for my shroud right now
is the world that loved me,
there's nothing my soul
should feel shame about.
MY BODY LIES AND ROTS
DOWN IN THE EARTH BELOW.

XII. While we rest

We are right at home
here among the rocks.
the two of us, friends,
getting right along,
Joane and Miren
among the cypresses,
rotting on and on and on.
At night the cypresses
look so very long!
When remains on a tomb
love like we do
there's no way their bones
can tell who is who.

Our mentor yesterday
told us many lies;
there is no learning
among the dead:
We can look
at his books
like the animals, mute,

ikusten dituen
goizaldean zeruak,
noragino diraden
jaditsiko primuak,
edo atzean hildoak,
goldeak markatuak.

Gure maisua izan da
esperantza gaiztoa.
Aspalditik da hori
gure amonatxoa;
Gustiz eztia da
beti bere ahoa;
baina gizarajoa
oso makal dago,
herbalkeriak joa;
Amonarik eztaukat;
horregatik otsoa
hurbildu zitzaidan niri,
makurturik lepoa.

XIII. Partiera

Atabute honetan ehortzirik nago.
Nire gainean lauza pisu bat baitago,
ezomendut bururik kampora jasoko;
izarretako keinu bateke ikusiko,
airerik hartuko
musu bat emango,
lorerik moztuko,
haragirik jango.
Eznaiz egon hobeki inun, hemen haino.
Eznaiz inola egundo,
belaunbiko jarriko.
Pozkarioa ezin liteke
jaditsi jada gorago.
Amorioak egun honetan
eztu niretzat balio.

stare at the morning sky,
or the tracks their cousins
may walk on,
or the furrows the plough
left behind.

Our best mentor
was futile hope.
For the longest time
she was our grandma;
honey drips perennial
from her sweet mouth,
But she is sick, withered,
the poor thing has shrunk;
her strength, her valor, are gone.
I no longer have a grandmother,
that's why the wolf
approached
tail down.

XIII. The Departure

Watch me lie here in this coffin.
A great heavy tombstone on me,
I know I won't ever raise my head,
nor see the stars above twinkling.
I won't take a breath,
kiss someone,
pick a flower,
take a bite.
Yet I've never felt better, anywhere.
I don't intend
to kneel and pray.
I've reached the summit
of my joy.
Love now is nothing
but a void.

Nire errai guztiak usteldu dirade:
Barrabilak, urgotzak, giltzurrunak ere.
Nire hezur oriak agirian daude.
Iluntasun honetan batera gaude.
Miren ta Joane;
bakarrik garade;
elkar dugu maite.
Baina halaz ere
ilunpea ta biok ezkara adiskide.
Airea izanik ilunpe,
argirik ezta batere;
eta begiek bihotzetara
heriotzea dakarte.
Heriotzea, amorioa,
ezin elkartu litezke.

Hezurrok egon dira hilobiz hilobi.
Gauza guztiak ditut jadanik ikusi.
Eztut nire bidean ezer erabaki;
eta gure aurrean munduak agiri,
hozen eta argi,
eder eta garbi.
Eta bihotzari
enadak, kantari.
Melodian esaten dizkio legunki.
Enada beltzak emeki
okotz honetan, ugari,
musu bigunak, laztangarriak,
eman zizkidan neroni:
Ezta sekula amorio bat
ezainagoa estali.

Moredinek eztute entzun ene kanta,
aginetatik irten didan hortz-garraska,
durrunduz erakusten duena ene kasta;
Etzen honen kexati izan gure aita;
etzen izan, baina
nire damua da
ta nire tristura,
iluntasuna ta
isiltasuna nire etsaiak baitira.

My entrails are all rotten:
even my testicles, kidneys, pancreas.
My yellow bones are on display.
And in this darkness together we lay.
Miren and Joane,
just us,
in love.
But even then
darkness is not our friend.
Shadows fill the air,
light is never there,
And eyes carry oblivion
into our hearts.
Death and love
can't be one.

Our bones roll around the tomb.
I think I have seen everything,
and along the way decided nothing.
For in front of us the world reveals,
loud and clear,
beautiful and clean.
And swallows sing into our heart,
sweet melodies
that prick the soul.
Black swallows kiss
my chin, my neck, peck
my soft places
with caresses.
Never did love
hush with more grace.

The blackberry bushes no longer hear my song,
nor the gnashing of my teeth,
which in itself reveals my origins;
my father didn't complain this much,
he didn't by far,
and it is my sadness
and my regret,
that darkness, silence,
are things I hate.

Lore guztiek eginka
edan zidaten odola;
haragasi-ustu ninduten gero
sagu bat banintz bazala,
(Haek katu bat bere aitarik
ez ezagutu duena).

Lauzak ene burua etzidan ukitu,
baina nire gainean du haunitz pisatu.
Nire presoia zela ezin dut ukatu,
naiz ta bazen hadikan astiro mugitu.
Mintzul eta mutu,
sogor eta itsu
geldi ta katigu,
orduan geratu
nintzen, inoiz harriak kemenik ezpaitu.
Harri lodia altzatu,
nire kateak apurtu;
Libertatea aho-zabalik
ederki nuen gozatu,
argi biziak nire begiak
zituenean urratu.

Biziak eman zigun seina bihotz eder;
eriotzeak bana ezkutuko bazter.
Kondenatu ginduten zentzuaren partez;
Urkamendira ginen biok joan artez,
geldiro ta nekez.
Ezkenuen hartzen
parterik han, zerren
gure borreroen
biotza zen humila, gogor, aratz, ustel . . .
Eta zeruan, nabarmen,
gure belaunak zurruntzen . . .
Ezta komeni, ene maitea,
hain bildurtiak izaten.
Enekin erdu; errautsak laga.
Lurpean gera etzaitez.

All the flowers
sucked my blood;
they gnawed at my flesh
as if I were a mouse,
(like orphaned cats
without a house).

The tombstone didn't touch my head,
but weighed heavily on me all the same.
It was my prison, I won't deny it,
although in time, it's true, it retracted.
Mum and mute,
deaf and blind,
still and captive
I remained,
the tombstone didn't care.
I pushed the slab up,
I broke my chains;
I gulped liberty
in great big gulps
when the light of life
pierced my eyes.

Life gave us each a beautiful heart,
death gave us both a place to hide.
We were sentenced without reason,
and together we suffered
a long slow sorrow imprisoned.
Our love couldn't
manifest then,
our tormentors' hearts
were small, hard, rotten,
a mirror of their God's;
and with time,
our knees collapsed.
My beloved, it's not good
to be so afraid.
Come with me,
leave those ashes.
Come up from under.

Eztut ene laguna iratzarri egun;
melodi atsegin hau etzaio ezagun.
Esaten diodanik eztit ezer entzun.
Borondatearekin egin diot eztul;
baina hain da zuhur,
hain da begi-makur,
hain da bihotz-legun,
ezen bere sudur
motzak eztuen egin usainik kontentuz.
Galdetu nion ze moduz,
arneguaren podesuz
hegaz eginik igan liteken
zeruetara Berzebud,
eta Jaunaren barkazioa
irabaz hantxe mosu-truk.

Hamar urte honetan eztut dantzan egin.
Ezta inor etorten batera nirekin.
Hemen gentzazin biok, errautsak itorik;
Gorputz hilok eztugu hartzen harnasarik.
Oraintxe badakit
ederki, zergatik
maite zaitudan nik.
Ene andre polit:
Zure ezagera etorri zait astiz.
Eta etzaude bizirik.
Zure usainak kendu dit
zugan jarrita neukan fedea,
Eztut igarten noizdanik
aingeruaren begitarteak
alde egin zuen zugandik.

Zure gorputza dago orain atinik hor:
usainik zakarrena kanporantza dator.
Eztut igarten nola naizen horrela egon,
itsusian sarturik, ederretik kanpoz.
Ongi derizkiot
zure arima motz
horri, zerren inoiz
aireak eztion
ezein gorputz hilari hain luzaro itxandon.

I haven't woken my woman still,
it seems she won't hear my melody,
my words mean nothing to her.
I even coughed softy,
But she's so careful,
so shy,
so tender of heart,
her little nose
can't detect the fragrance of my hope.
I asked, blasphemously, if
we could fly to Satan's crib
and earn the pardon of God
in exchange for a kiss.

I haven't danced in ten years,
no one danced with me.
Here we lay choked with ashes;
dead bodies that don't flex muscles.
Now I know
well why
I loved you so,
my beauty:
I had all the time to know you
while you weren't alive.
Your stench killed
my faith in you.
I can't even recall
when the angel in your face
left your skull.

There lies your body, face up,
exuding the most horrendous odor,
And I stay there, I don't notice,
entrenched in the ugly, away from all beauty.
I know so well that soul of yours
locked up for so long
in the atmosphere of a corpse.
I kick my way out of there.
I'm finally out for good.

Bulzatu naute ostikoz.
Kanpoan nago betikotz.
Eremu hori izan da beti
harrixka artean txit elkor,
eta euritea datorrenean
orduan ere bai legor.

Erori da behera berriz lauz-harria
estaldurik betiko neure maitalea,
lore-mendian hartu neuen begonia,
hainbat maitatu nuen Mirentxo maitea,
dontzella garbia,
ukitu-gabea,
hibaiko lorea,
mendiko txoria.
Eta dolore haundiz datorkit airea
esanik: Hator, librea;
ezagut hezak hodeia:
horrek eztakik mundua dela
haundia eta zelaia?
Baina bihotza, errauts eginik,
han zen geratu, tristea.

Zimaur bortitzarekin landuriko ortua,
honek oparo digu emanen frutua,
ta da udaberrian guztiz loratua.
Hort gertatu zaigu. Gu bezalakoa
delako mundua.
Da Miren gozoa,
Joane baitoa
ihesi. Onartua
izan bedi zimaurra, benedikatua.
zerren bestela zerua
izanen zaigun galdua,
ta zerumuga ezagutzeko
daukat gurari gertua:
Eznaiz biziko, zapaldu arte
zeruetako zolua.

This place among the rocks
was always dry and barren,
even with the rain,
it never held water.

The tombstone fell down again,
encasing my lover forever,
the lily I picked on the flower mountain,
little Miren I loved so much,
the purest damsel,
untouched,
my river flower,
my mountain bird.
And filled with sorrow the wind
beckons: come, come now that you're free!
Come meet the cloud,
don't you know the expanse
of the world and the sky?
But my heart, a sad mound of ashes,
stayed buried with her inside.

Soil enriched with much sap
shall bear fruit in abundance
and bloom with flowers in the spring.
And so it was. Because
the world is like us.
Sweet Miren alone,
and Joane escaping away
and beyond. Embrace
then, the sap, blessed be,
since otherwise we risk
the loss of all that's heavenly,
and the line of the horizon ahead
calls and I can't wait
until I know the feel
of heaven's ground beneath my feet.

XIV. Arbuioaren bitartez

Ukitzen nauten eskuek
naramate gorantza.
Behera erorteko
eztaukat esperantza;
horixe ertatu
zitzaidan herrirantza;
nindoanean, antza.
Eztute ezagutu
neronen mendekantza.
Eztut estimatuko
beren adiskidantza,
arima pisua baitut,
ta noa beherantza.

Nire etsaien eskuak
usain zikinok dira,
eskeintzen didatenak
orain munduko jira;
eta joan behar dut
Eldorado berrira:
Egiazko Palmira
horretan diamante,
opaloak balira,
harri preziatuak
ederrenak baitira,
eznintzake itzuliko
inoiz lore-mendira.

Urregorrizko etxean
hadago edertasuna,
baina berunezkoan
tristura bat, astuna,
edozein gizoni
demona behaztuna.
Hau da nire fortuna,
egunero galtzen
nauen mingotasuna.
Hori da egunotan

XIV – In Rejection

The hands clasping me
carry me up.
It's hopeless
to think of descent;
The same happened
on my journey home,
the familiarity of it.
They never knew
the revenge I sought.
their excuses mean nothing,
my soul weighs
and I'm falling.

The hands of my enemies
smell of something rotten,
they are the same ones
that caused my ascent;
but I must go
seek a new El Dorado:
the true city of Palmyra,
land of diamonds and opals,
and other most precious
among the precious gems.
I can never return
to the flower mountain.

There is beauty
in the golden mansion,
and in the lead one,
a sadness, a weight,
that is for the human
an impediment.
This is my fate,
the bitterness
that corrodes me every day.
The knowledge

galazitzen diguna
elkarrekin egotea.
Hau da garraztasuna!

XV. Judizioa

Arima penatuak afusilatuko
dituzte arratsaldean. Eta belaunbiko
Goya miragarri bat kemen gabe dago;
eta bere kapela zuen erauntziko
burutsik balego.
Ongi jauntzi, edo
dotoretu gero,
daduzkan soineko
apainekin. Arima penatuak dio:
Hori ezpaita inoizko,
ez uzti, bada geroko.
Fusil haueri joran bizian
egon natzaie espero.
Nire tristura ezin liteke
erori jada berago.

Nire etsai zikinek juntatu gaituzte,
baina hilerrietan separatu dute
gure amorioa, ezpaita posible
arimak maitatzea gorputzikan gabe.
Hau delako gure
asturua, triste:
kaliza hau bete
gainez egin arte.
Bidegabe honekin eznago konforme.
Mundua ezta alegre:
eztut ukatu beinere
eztakit ongi zergatik eman
nuen bizia hain merke;
orain eznuke mendira igoko
nire etsaiak hil gabe.

Etsaien kontra nago erruz arnegari,
eman zidatelako ondiko ugari.

that we are forbidden
from togetherness.
Oh yes, the bitterness!

XV. The Judgment

The condemned will face
the firing squad in the afternoon.
A Goyaesque man on his knees, done,
He would take his cap off,
if only he had one,
or if he were well dressed, or more
elegantly, with the fine clothes
he owns. The condemned soul says:
since this is the end anyway,
please don't delay.
I am ready to put my life
before this rifle.
My sadness
has nowhere to go.

My vile enemies brought us together,
but separated our love at the grave,
because disembodied souls
cannot love.
And this is our sad luck:
fill the goblet
to the top,
let it spill.
I don't agree with what happened to me.
I never denied
the world isn't happy,
but why didn't I
sell my life at a higher price.
I wouldn't climb that mountain now,
not without killing my enemy first.

My burning fury is for my enemies,
they've given me reason enough.

Aingeru Serafinek akerra dirudi,
deabru Belialek epetxa kantari.
Eta Dostoiefskii
jaio ezpaledi,
eznioke Prousti
barkatuko hori:
Zergatik gizonari eztion jarraiki.
Picassok ere Goyari
kentzen dizkio humilki
mundu honetan bizi izateko
izan zituen gurari
guztiak, eta beste hainbeste
gertatzen zaio Mozarti.

Bihotzean sarturik daukat mendekantza:
Picasso, Proust ta Bartok damutuko dira.
Hasarre haundiz noa orain haiengana,
besapean zuzia, eskuan haizkora,
ahoan labaña
eta gañibea.
Hau da nire harma
poteretsuena:
Saihets-artean dudan arbuio sakona.
Honekin diat bihotza
erdibituko nik, eta
egunsentia datorrenean,
Gernika balitz bezala,
Parnaso berri hori negarrez
orduan geratuko da.

Heldu nintzen haraino, eta begiratu
nion nire bizitza hain doilorki hartu
zidan eskribau hari, eta nuen damu,
hain jente makur hura bainuen tratatu.
Mendekantzak ditu
hamar mila musu
eun mila ta piku
begitarte mutu:
Eta nik bat bakarra behar dut hautatu.
Gizon guztiek arnegu
egiten dute: Adizu!

The angel Seraphim is a billy goat,
and the demon Belial a lowly wren.
Had Dostoyevsky
never been born,
I wouldn't know
how to forgive Proust:
why didn't he follow the man.
Picasso himself humbly stole
Goya's every desire
to live in this world,
and so did Mozart.

My heart is set on revenge:
Picasso, Proust, and Bártok will regret.
I walk toward them in fury,
A torch and an axe, one per hand,
knife and switch blade
in mouth.
And my most dangerous weapon:
the enormous contempt my rib cage contains.
It will break their hearts in two,
and at first light of dawn,
that new Parnassus
will melt into tears,
just like Gernika did.*

I arrived there and stared
at the scribe who did so easily decide
to undo my life, and damned him.
I regretted entertaining such lowlifes.
Revenge poses
ten thousand grins,
and more than a hundred thousand
silent squints.
But I must choose one single semblance.
All men shout at me:
Hey! Are you just avenging

Zure maitea mendekatzeko
gura bakarra dakarzu
edo naiago duzu dirutan
egin duguna kobratu?

Hauzi zakar hau ezta konponduko legez.
Honela uste duenak egiten du amets.
Mendekantzok irteten didate aldrebes.
Goizaldean bazkaldu nahi nuen plater
bete bihotz ustel,
apaltzeko gibel
batzuk oso zimel.
Orain eztakit zerk
sabel-darraio zirdin hau didan ekarten.
Gora-galea ematen
didate beti gizonek,
ta batez ere arratsaldean
sakon lo egin ondoren,
zerren orduan karitatean
eztut egundo pentsatzen.

Zerk bultzatu ginduen eztugu jakin guk,
zueri gu jasoten itsusiki gurutz
artez hartan, ta guri, indarrek ukatuz,
amore ematen: eta ongi dakit egun,
edo ezagutzen dut,
eginikan zurrust,
ezin duzula zuk
arima para zut,
zeren niri gertatu zitaiden hau erruz.

Arnoarekin hordituz,
edo gaznekin asetuz,
ezin liteke inolaz ere
zede gerturik ezagut,

the woman you loved?
Isn't it better that you demand
repairs for what they did?

Laws won't fix this absurd process,
believing that is a mess.
There's a problem with my revenge.
I wanted to breakfast
on a rotten heart,
and for lunch eat
a liver past its best.
And now I don't know what
caused my stomach to ache.
Men always make me sick,
especially past noon,
after a siesta lull,
because by then
my forgiveness is gone.

We never understood
what pushed you to crucify us;
why we let you do it,
why we denied our power.
And today I've come
to understand that the soul
can't stand upright
when drink soaks it up.
Blurred with wine,
filled with cheese,
there's no way
your limits are clear,
because, as bodies dance,
souls drown.

Kneel! If you don't,
I will follow you
from death's dark realm
and beyond,

arima itotzen baita, gorputza
dagoenean kontentuz.
Belaunika zaitezte! Edo bestela nik,
heriotze osteko eremu beltzetik
pausu geldiarekin honera etorririk,
eztizuet emanen batere etsedenik.
Nago penaturik;
ezta arimarik
nekatuagorik
agertzen inundik,
eztare infernuetan kondenatzen denik.
Para zaitezte zutirik!
Etzakuskitet damurik.
Eztakizue zuek egiten
nire aurrean otoitzik?
Gauza egokia da hori beti
denarentzako bizirik.

Haek zeuden negarrez, igurikitzen noiz
deskargatuko nuen haizkora hain zorrotz
hura beren buruen gainean, zerren bost
urtean egon ziren nire, zai, ondikoz
beterik. Hamabost
eliz-, lege-gizon,
erlojeru, arotz,,
errementari motz,
alkate, nekazari, eta igeltseru on.
Nire inguruan guztiok
zeuden negarrez: Tristeok,
ai, gure triste, esaten, zuten,
ai, gure gajo, pobreok!
Eztigutela zendu artean
pazienteki itxadon.

Zeru gorena dago hodeiez betea.
Gure barnean ere badago hodeia.
Fabore ian genuen orduan legea;
orain apurtu dute gure kodizea.
Epal-emalea
datorkigu, ea

steadily, without pause.
I am drowning in sorrow;
a lost soul, so lost,
no one can follow,
not even the condemned,
those who inhabit the circles of hell.
Stand up!
You show no remorse.
Can't you pray before me?
Praying is good,
all live things should.

They all cried, dreading the moment
my merciless axe came
down on their heads.
They'd waited five years:
five years in fear of my return.
Fifteen men:
Lawyers and monks,
watchmakers, carpenters,
a brute of a blacksmith,
mayors, farmers, and bricklayers.
All around me they cried,
they lamented: oh poor us!
poor us! they said,
oh how unfortunate we are,
see how patience, in the end,
wasn't on our side.

Clouds menace the skies above,
and cloud us inside too.
Laws once shielded us,
but the codex broke.
A judge
approaches,

nolako fedea
daukugun. Gurea
erabakita dago. Astuna nekea!
Gizona izanik txikia,
adimentua hertsia,
ezin pentsatu baitezakegu
zein den izanen amaia,
eztezaigula ezer ofrezi
ezpada herotzea.

Egunean iraulten egon da gorua,
erramu freskoekin eginez koroa,
apainduko didena goforki burua,
ezten inor ni bezain ohoreztatua.
Gauean dornua
eztago lotua:
Nai dute estatua
bat oso haltua
herriko plazan jaso, benedikatua
izan dedila maisua,
gaur dagoena itoa
hainbeste jente artean, eta
baita harnasa kendua,
zerren jainkoak baino askozaz
da bera prestuagoa.

XVI- Adorazioaren bitartez

Amaitu ginen lekuan
egin dute kapera.
Ezta pentsatzekoa
gizonen bukaera:
Erori zitzaigun
apurturik lurrera
apurturik urrera
jan genuen platera
mila zatitan. Dut
ezpondatik atera
erregalatu nizun

to check the limits
of our faith.
The verdict is clear,
and painful to bear!
The smallness of humans,
their walled-in worlds,
their inability to see
what awaits in the beyond,
other than death
and its meaninglessness.

All day the loom turned and turned,
my crown with fresh flowers bloomed,
looking pretty on my head,
such honor, such blessings I received.
Nights' quiet
isn't kept:
Someone wants a statue
built in the square,
a tall one, to bless
the teacher
who today chokes
amid so much flesh,
trying, every day
to earn the favor
of every God on earth.

XVI. In Adoration

They've built a chapel
on top of our grave.
We tend
not to contemplate the end:
The plate
from which we ate
slipped and fell
and like that
a million fragments became.
So I brought your silverware
out

zilarrezko baxera:
Erlikitzat egun dute
eraman aldarera.

Zure memoriak egin
dituzte gaur elizan,
eznadien hasarra
ostopo baten gisan.
Ezti-makatza da
aurkitua kalizan
asturugaizki izan.
Eztute ezein gauza
deseginen astiz han,
espantuz eta urduri
dabiltzalako prisan.
Hilen dira, berenua
dagoelako zizan.

Ezritu penarik eman
hotikan ikusteak
barkazio gabeko
kondena-gai tristeak?
Niri bai, haundia.
Eztiotsu legeak
erreinuko erregeak
hil behar duela,
zerren bere andreak
adar haundiak jarri
dizkio, bai, luzeak?
Eztizu ajolarik izan
gizon-kondenatzeak?

XVII. Mendakantza

Elizatzar honetan orain ezpanego,
elitzaidake inola gogora etorriko
zure oroitzapenik edo geratuko
litzake lore gabe etor zedineko.
Barren edo kanpo,
garratz edo gozo,

from the ground.
Like a relic
it sits on the altar.

Your funeral oration
was sung today in mass
to keep me calm
and avoid any contratemps.
A poached pear
miraculously filled
the holy chalice.
They weren't able
to undo a thing,
and now they're nervous,
afraid, moving too fast.
The cup is poisoned
and they will die.

Isn't it pitiful to watch
fate relentlessly approach
those poor,
condemned men?
It is, very.
Don't the laws say
the king of the kingdom
must be executioner,
and avenge
his wife,
the adulterer?
Isn't it pitiful that man
always condemns himself?

XVII. The Revenge

It's only because I'm in this church
you've invaded my thoughts,
there'd be no flowers or memory
were I not in this scenery.
Inside or out,
bitter or sweet,

eztu pausatuko,
ez oheratuko,
Nire memori onak ezin daidike lo.
Nire negarrak eztio
kontsoluari deituko.
Ene maitea ene laztana,
zu gaberikan eztago
mundu honetan zori gaiztoan
alaitasunik neutzako.

Etzaitezte, mesedez, orain hainbat pobre.
Zuen bihotz urria aberats zazue.
Letaria hauekin lasai etzaudete.
Haragidun gizona benetan da triste.
Eztauka batere
egiazko fede
edo karitate:
guztia da atzipe.
Zerura jadisteko esperantzak ere.
Miren eztago presente,
betiko dago ausente.
Zuen otoitzok eta erreguok
egiaz dira debalde.
Urrikalmentu gizon-zalerik
eztut inola nik gorde.

Etzaitezte, pobreok, oraintxe defendi;
nire goikotasuna eztadin ofendi;
dezazuen ederki zer naizen entendi;
dezazuen agintzen dudana obedi;
honera nator ni,
haltu eta haundi,
bortitz eta egoki.
Errezatzen hari
zarate, gero nadin zuetzat urriki.
Ezer ez eska Jaunari!
Biotza daukat hain urri . . .
Zuekandikan eznabil-eta
egun honetan ihesi,
nire haizkora, nire arbuioa,
doazkizue hegazi.

it won't stop,
it won't rest in bed with me,
my memory can't sleep.
It's not solace
my tears seek.
My darling my love
I can't find joy
in this world,
without you there's none.

Don't please feel sorry for yourself now,
you may still fill your heart.
This litany just won't do.
This man of flesh is a sad spectacle,
he owns no true faith,
no true charity:
he knows it all
to be false,
even his hope to ascend the heavens.
Because Miren isn't there,
but her absence is, always.
Your prayers, your supplications
are in vain.
I can't take pity
on men.

So don't try to defend yourselves, you misers,
you cannot offend my grandiosity,
try hard to understand my return,
and obey, do as you're told;
I came here
glorious, noble,
strong and remote.
Pray to me
so I may take pity on you.
Don't ask anything of the Lord!
My heart is so far from here,
I'm not with you,
I'd much rather run,
and leave you
with my axe and my disdain.

Nire hustasunaren barnean, harrika,
heiagoraz, egiten nuen gogoeta;
nolako gastigua zen egokiena
nire borreroari emateko; eta
ezin nuen petsa
beste ezin gauza:
Talion izanen da!
Behar dut babesa.
Barnean duten oro nai diet atera.
Hau da zuentzat morrontza:
nire hitzari egonda,
ezin igarri zein den emanen
zaitzuen azken parada.
Enetxo, zuek urrikarriok,
banaukazue prest jada.

Orduan hasi nuen, gogor eta itsu,
nire burrukaldia: geratzeko kitu.
Beren larruetatik arin nintzen sartu,
eta errai guztiak nizkien altzatu:
Garunea kendu,
hesteak ohostu,
bihotza zabaldu,
giltzurrunak moztu;
gizonaren bularrak labirintu bat du.
Baina eznintzen ez, galdu:
gauza guztiak aurkitu
nituen beren leku gertuan,
eta kanpora botatu
nituen denak, erroiek izan
lezaten nundik gizendu.

Arimaren erraiak ebatsi nizkien,
pena litezen denak munduan dolorez.
Fede, karitatea, esperantza kentzen
ausartu nintzen nire nekearen ordez.
Badakit kobratzen,
baina dirutan ez.
Deabruak, erren,
egiten du amets:
Erroiaren antzean ederki da asetzen.

As stones rained silently on me
and I screamed, I considered
what punishment would befit
my tormentors;
I could think
of nothing else.
Nothing would placate me but
an eye for an eye,
I made up my mind.
I wanted everything they have inside.
That's your punishment:
you won't know
when your last truce comes.
My morons, I am ready.

So I went for them, hard and blind;
it was my fight, an immeasurable fight.
I pierced their skin quickly,
and tore away their entrails.
I emptied their brains,
stole their intestines,
opened their hearts,
cut out their kidneys.
The chest of man is a labyrinth,
but I never got lost:
everything was
in its rightful place
and everything I pulled out
and threw around
to fatten the crows.

I pulled out the animals' entrails
to watch them suffer in agony.
I removed their faith, charity, their hope,
to soothe my existential exhaustion.
I know how to collect,
although money isn't my object.
The devil too
knows how to dream:
like a crow, he happily eats his fill.

Inorl eztaki negarrez
bere garaitza hospatzen.
Gizon etoiak hutsitu ditut
mendekantzaren ohorez.
Hoiek Mireni zioten zorra
kitatu diet ongien.

Burrukaldi haundia gaur irabazi dut;
etsaien harmadurak errez hautsi ditut.
Eta nire nekea ezin direke neurt.
Eskumako belauna daukat bogei apur.
Egin diot agur
lehen neukan gorputz
osoari. Ta gaur
eztakit jada deus,
ezpada eztaukadala ezein saihets-ezur.
Aginak galdu dira erruz.
Okotza ere bertan utz.
Nire zauriak sendatutzeko
jezarri nintzen atabut
baten gainean, malda gorea
eztadin izan hain biluz.

Begiratu ere nuen gatazka-lekutik,
eta eznuen ikusi batere hilotzik.
Ezta egon gizona inoiz hain bizirik:
ni hil arte ezta egon halako gizonik,
hain bizitzen denik.
Eztute nekerik,
daudelako hutsik.
Merezi nuen nik
eskerrak lizkidaten bihotz-bihotzetik.
Orain eztago itzalik.
Ezta zeruan goibelik.
Beren aurrean ezta kausitzen
lehengo behatz-toporik.
hoek ibili litezke orain
sufritu gabe mundutik.

Nire hezurretako zauritzar sakonok
medikuntza-legean ezin dira konpon.

And so it is with victory,
nobody thinks to cry.
But I have killed traitorous men
seeking to avenge a debt.
I honored Miren
and those who owed her, paid.

I won an old battle today;
I crushed my enemies' armor,
until I almost crashed with exhaustion.
My knee broke in twenty places,
and I said goodbye
to the body that I had.
And all I know,
my only certainty,
is that forever I must lack a rib.
My teeth are gone,
and I think my jaw broke.
I sat on a coffin
to lick my wounds,
and make the uphill struggle
less raw.

I looked at the battlefield again,
and didn't see a single corpse:
No man ever felt more alive,
nor did a dead man
ever live a fuller life.
The others suffer nothing,
because inside, they're hollow.
I deserve
their heartfelt gratefulness.
all shadows are gone,
all the darkness from the clouds.
All the obstacles they faced,
they are no longer there.
Now they can roam the world
and never suffer.

No medicine can heal
the deep wounds of my bones,

Materia zikina bertatik zerion.
Adiskide mamia nendukan Derion,
mutiko guztiz on,
hemen balitz egon . . .
Eznengoke pasmoz
zikindurik inoiz.
Sendatuko balizkit oraingo zauriok . . .
Falta zaizkidan hezurrok
eztira ikusten lurreaon.
Gora begira nire begiak
ikusten dute derrigor,
zer zen jazoko gizon artera
haizkora gabe banentor.

Eta ikusten dute han goian bestia,
lengo gizon beteek hamorruz jarria,
oraingo gizon hutsek bera jaurtikia,
hamiltegui batean azkar eroria,
lepo ebakia,
buru itzulia,
hatzamar gabea,
agin aterea,
antolatzen duela infernu berria.
Ahora dator barrea,
ezpainetara irria.
Errez izan da hinguinduaren
harmak lurrera jotea.
Ehortz dezagun bein da betiko
gizasemeen etsaia!

Nire gorputza eta odol berotsua . . .
Hezur batzuk oraindik . . . ezpaiten naikoa
Hau da gizonakandik dakardan kontua
Gizateria izan dadin salbatua.
Naizela maisua . . .
Gauean itsua . . .
Badator ordua!
Nire erlojua . . .
Oraindikan aldean baitaukat burua!
Bildots berria, mantsoa;
Jainko bortitza, haltua:

which suppurate and ooze.
I had a dear friend in Derio,
really a good guy,
if only he were here . . .
I wouldn't be in such a state,
frozen into place.
If only he could cure me!
The bones I am missing
are not of this earth.
That's why I'm forced
to look elsewhere and up,
I don't know what would happen
if I went among men with my hatchet.

I see the other one up there,
they put him up there in anger,
and they, the same hollow men,
pushed him down the precipice, into the abyss,
and his neck broke,
his head turned,
he lost fingers,
he lost teeth,
a new hell formed.
Laughter fills my mouth,
a smile stretches my lips.
How easily the fallen
let go of every weapon.
Let's bury now and forever
this cruel enemy of men.

My body and warm blood . . .
a number of my bones . . . they weren't enough!
This is the check men will have me pay
to save humanity's day.
They call me mentor . . .
a blind man in the night . . .
my hour is nigh!
My watch . . .
my head held still high!
I am a new, docile lamb;
a mighty, powerful God:

Zuri eskerrak, ordu honetan
dago geugana heldua
joran bizian eduki nahi
genuen salbamentua.

XVIII. Grinaren bitartez

Nire maitalea dago
etzanda lauza-pean.
Bestiarik eztago
ezein duda gabe han
Garbia da dena
Mirenen gorputzean.
Piztu dadin artean.
Hilotzen artetik
jaiki dadin artean.
Ezta gutiziarik
beraren bihotzean.
Zein ederki egoten den
maitearen aldean!

Joane dago indar gabe
gizonari begira.
Sakon sartu zitzaidan
bihotzean kupira.
Munduko gizonak
manaiakorrak dira.
Esaten diet: Tira!
Ta tiratzen dute,
hau da nire kadira,
ilunpeko txinparta
guztietan distira.
Zein pozik bihurtzen naizen
orain lore-mendira!

Zer eginen zenuke zuk
hegaztina bazina?
Kabiarik eznuke
ezpamintz hegaztina.
Etxean sarturik

by virtue of your grace
today we received
the salvation
we sought.

XVIII. In Passion

My beloved lies
under a slab.
No doubt she's there
with no one.
Miren's body
is everything that's holy.
Until she returns
from the dead,
until she resurrects.
There is no want
in her heart.
How beautiful she looks
next to the one she loves!

Joane looks at the man,
his strength all gone.
Deep in his heart
compassion awoke.
The men of this world
are really so docile.
You tell them: pull!
and they pull.
Here I stand
shining bright
with the sparks in the dark.
I am so happy to go back
to the flower mountain!

What would you do
if you were bird?
If I could fly
I'd have no nest.
Deep in my house

dadukat bake fina.
Etzara pospolina
Baina bai hamabi
ostoko krabelina.
Nire Miren maiteak
dirudi erregina.
Dotoreki sartu zidan
harenganako mina.

XIX. Azkenengo besarkada

Mirenen maitasuna daukat haltuago
zerupean dagoen ezein gauza baino.
munduko gizadia salbatunk dago.
Orain ezta problema, ezta misterio,
Joanerentzako:
argitan dago oro,
agiri ta klaro.
Eta guretzako
airean ibiltea hegazi da naiko.
Ai, ene Miren inungo!
Zure gorputza nun dago?
Atsegin guzti guztien madre
orijinala, gorago
zure imajina altzatutzeko
palankarikan eztago.

Nire zauri gordinak sendaturik gabe,
handikan jaiki nintzen, zerren ezta nire
gurari nagusia ezergatik ere
bakarrik egotea. Hori da debalde.
Maitea nun zaude?
Negar egin dute
larrosek, ez barre.
estea da beste.
Usainen akorduek hara naramate:
Ez emanikan amore,
oro ukatzen didate.
Hara joateko dagozkit hoek

lives lovely peace.
You're no dove,
but a twelve-petal
rose.
Miren my love
is a queen.
How sweetly
I came to feel her pain.

XIX. The Last Embrace

I hold Miren's love in higher esteem
than anything that exists under heaven's keep.
Humanity has been saved:
there is no problem now,
no mystery.
To Joane,
everything is in the light,
revealed, clear.
And all we need
is to fly freely in the sky.
Oh Miren, you are nowhere and everywhere!
Where did your body go?
You were the root
of my every joy.
Nothing I can say
can praise you enough.

I left that place in a rush,
my wounds still unhealed,
what I desired the most
was to be no longer alone.
But it didn't happen so.
Where are you my love?
Don't laugh,
look how the roses cry.
They are not the only ones.
The memory of scents carried me there,
but it was all for nothing,
they denied me everything.

birtute bigun bi galde,
ta baldin nire hezurrak hausten
bazaizkit ere bai eske.

Ta urrats geldiarekin haratza noa ni,
nire kontra datorren hizean iherri;
pisuarekin ere nago burrukari.
Mirenek itxadoten didala baneki . . .
Baina etzait hori
gustatzen neroni:
oraintxe hezur bi
lurrerat erori . . .
Honela ezin liteke aurrerantza segi!
Eznaiz atzela itzuli;
eztut indarrik eduki,
altzipresaren kerizpe beltzak
ikusten ditut hurruti:
Haraginoko indarrek izan
beharko dute geiegi!

Eztut orain artean bilatu nun pausa,
bidearen luzea eztakidan luza.
Bidearen dagoena ezta nire gauza:
Nire asmoa izan da hobiaren lauza
gogorkiro altza
baldin al banenza
oraintxe gorantza.
Baina hori ezta
hilerrira nakarren zapore garratza.
Haragi gabe, han dentza
nire Mirenen gorputza:
al banintzake nire hezurrak
hezur hoietan deskantsa . . . !
Hau da benetan eskapu gabe
gora naraman ametsa.

Har-lauzaren azpira nuen begiratu,
emanik lehenbizi errautsean musu;
Miren nuen honela auspez adoratu;
bere beratz-artea ere milikatu

And my weak virtue demands
that I go on and seek,
even if my bones are crushed
even if my strength resists.

And slowly, very slowly I walk on,
floating on the air that holds me,
pushing against it as I scramble.
If only I could be certain Miren awaited me!
But I am not liking
what is happening:
Two more bones
have just fallen off me . . .
How can I keep going!
There's no way I'm returning;
I have no more strength,
I see the shadows
the cypresses cast over there.
I must harness my power
and keep going over.

I haven't yet taken a break,
I don't want the road to stretch ahead.
The journey is not my concern,
what I want is to find her grave,
and free the slab
that seals her sepulcher,
lift it up, push it far.
Even if it's hard.
But it's not this that embitters my walk,
but the thought of the body of my beloved,
all fleshless, all bone.
If only my bones
could rest with her bones.
It is only these dreams
that allow me to push on.

I looked intently under the tombstone
and kissed the ashes first of;
in this way I adored her,
I kissed her every toe,

nai nuen, setatsu;
oin-zolak ukitu,
orpoak laztandu,
belaunak topatu:
Hamabost egunean bertantxe geratu.
Bere ankartea maitatu,
eta gerria berotu;
bere petxua behin egon zen
saihets-ezurrak hotzitu,
ta bere agin zuri-zuriak
hamorru haundiz apurtu.

Harria gora jaso bedi, esan nuen.
Bihotza taupadaka, begiak negarrez.
Eta eznuen aurkitu barrenean ezer!
Iharrausi ninduen gertaera harek,
nire buruaren
barnean dolorez.
Hermita hau leher
bezate trumoiek!
Eror bedi lurrera ahalik lasterren!
Aurrerantzean inoiz ez!
Ezpedi torre hau ager
gure memori flakoan, eta
salbatu diren gizonek
Jaungoikoari dieten zorra
paga bezate halaxen,

Eznenkien zer egin, arima nun ortus;
munduan daudelako mila ta bat gorputz;
zapatarikan gabe, guztiak zapalduz
Mirenen bila joan behar dut arneguz.
Hau da nire gurutz
pisuena! Jesus!
Jainko gabe zeruz
zeru gurutzatuz!
Nire desesperantzat esperantza dakus.
Inoiz eznezan bertan utz!
eskatu nion, humilduz,
lore-mendian, ta baita ere
golgota-mendian, hain biluz

everything that was soft,
caressed her feet,
cradled her heels,
came up to her knees,
and stayed there two weeks.
I loved the space between her legs,
warmed her waist,
rearranged the ribs
that once hosted her tits,
and with all my might
broke her white teeth.

Lift the lid, I heard myself say,
my heartbeat wild,
floods in my eyes.
But there was nothing inside!
Something happened then
and my head burst
with blood and with pain.
May thunder
shatter this chapel!
May it crumble, may it collapse!
May the memory of it vanish
from our shallow minds,
and may the men who were saved
pay the heavenly debt they owe
in this terrible way.

My soul barefoot, knew not what to do;
of so many bodies the world is full,
and they walk with or without shoes.
I must search for Miren, I must go.
This is my cross.
Jesus, this is the worst!
I am crossing the heavens
without a God!
In my hopelessness, hope pulsated.
Don't leave me here alone!
I begged humbly,
not in the flower mountain,
and not in the desert either.

haretan. Eta joan nintzelako
doekit orain mendekuz.

Bizirik eztuena ezin liteke hil.
Baina honera ezkero eztut hori jakin.
Mirenen heiagora hodeietan dabil.
Nire oroitzapenak barnean dauka min.
Alegre banenbil
batera harekin . . .
Mundua biribil,
konprenitu-ezin.
Paradisu bat nahi dut, han gaitezen bil!
Egintza bakan hontan, nik
eztakust argibiderik.
Bere krobitxet zuri garbia
lohi zikinez beterik
lurrean datza, eta negarrez
goratu nueh bertatik.

Malda gorea dago nire aurrean, hor.
Gizona nintzenean sei urtean egon
nintzen eremuearen akordua dator
nire gogora, eta intzirinaz diot:
Bazekiat gogoz
hire bide zihor
guztiak nola igon.
Berak berriz diost:
Ausart hadi etorten; begira natzegok.
Hariztiraino heltzekotz
urteak dira hamabost.
Harantza noa, zerren Mirenen
hezurrak dauden mendion,
bide bateko sinale batzuk
harantza naramatenok.

Eznaute enteratu zein den mugarria,
nun bukatuko zaidan hemengo bidea,
zein den Mirenek hartu duen portalea.
Bainan eztit ajola: nire guraria,
nire gustizia,

And I think, this is her revenge,
she left because I left first.

If you're not alive you can't really die.
Up until now I hadn't really thought of that.
Miren's lament echoes through the clouds
and pain burrows deep into my thoughts.
If only I could be happy
and she with me . . .
The world is a circle,
and really incomprehensible.
I want a paradise, and us together there.
But nothing can
guide me in this endeavor.
Her clean white shroud
lay there, full of dirt,
on the ground.
I rescued it
with tears running down my cheeks.

I face the uphill slope ahead
and recall my time as man,
and my six years in the desert,
and angry I shout:
I know well
where your many
treacherous paths go.
And he replies in turn,
"I dare you: come, I'm waiting."
Fifteen years to the Oakwood
that's how long it takes.
And there's where I'm headed,
because Miren's bones await.
I know they're in the mountain,
signs will guide me there.

I still don't see the frontier, a rock
that marks the limit, the journey's end,
Miren's resting place.
But I don't mind: my will,
my desire, win,

laster gozatzea
da nire maitea,
zeinen aupegia
oihal aberatseon dakadan jarria.
Bera da Salbatorea,
ni Beronika berria.
Birjina Miren dultze gozoa
gurutze bati josia,
zeru berrira igon zenuen:
Hauxe da nire gloria!

Azkenengo mendia: badakust ortua.
Atzean da betiko arbola sikua.
Bidean utzi dugu gure arrastoa.
Nahi duena gure atzean bijoa!
Banaiz nekatua,
ta dolaratua!
Mendia haltua,
gizona flakoa . . .
Honera datorrena eztela zimua!
Azpian daukat mundua.
Ez goian berriz zerua.
Hezurrik gabe azkar erori
zait orain nire burua:
aire naizela haize batean
Mirenen bila banoa.

XX. Ditxaren bitartez

Besarkada eder batez
orain juntatu gara;
horregatikan
igan nintzen zeruetara.
Gertatu nahi dut
egiazko aldara;
badaukagu nun para.
Ezkontza berri bat
dezakegun prepara.
Haizeak bera dauka
barrenean ikara,
etortzekoa delako
orain gure elizara.

I shall soon
enjoy my lover
whose face
contours this fine cloth.
She's my Savior,
I am Veronica returned.
Sweet Virgin Miren
nailed to the cross,
you ascended to Heaven:
your glory is in me!

The last mountain: there's the garden.
Behind it the old dead tree.
Our footsteps still mark the way.
Let them follow if they wish!
I'm tired,
and I'm in pain!
High is the mountain,
weak is the man . . .
A chimp wouldn't reach here.
The world is at my feet,
and all the heavens above me.
My boneless head
falls easy:
I'm air in the wind
while Miren I seek.

XX – In Joy

We came together in a beautiful embrace
and that's the only reason
why I ascended the heavens.
I want to remain
on this altar of truth,
this place of ours.
Let us get married again.
The wind
sounds fearful,
it whistles
as it blows into church.

Mundutarrek adoratu
bagaitutze ere, nola
suntsituko da gure
maitasunaren zola?
Oneriztea da
guretzako kaiola,
eta burnizko bola;
bihotz berriotan
dirakien odola,
eta paradisuan
sustraitu den arbola.
Gainerakoak eztigu
ezergatik ajola.

Ahatzi dugu guztia
lurrean genkiena:
Ni ta zu hitzak, eta
gurea ta zuena;
larruko laketa
ta amaren ditiena:
Maria Matxalena,
Maria Birjina;
azpikoa, gorena.
Orain bat gara biok:
Adarra ta txortena.
Arraza berri bateko
animali lehena.

XXI. Malda gora eginiko gogoeta eroak

Zimiorik zatuienak,
utzi ditu zuhatzak,
Hibaiondoko haretan,
markaturik behatzak.
Arrokartean gizonak,
ematen ditu urratsak.

Orduan heldu zitzaien,
jaunaren aingerua.
Jan zazu amaren ugatza

Even if they adored us
down below,
where will the root
of our love grow?
Their adoration
is our prison,
our ball and chain:
the blood that flows
in hearts anew,
the tree that soaks
the sap of a new paradise.
The rest
is nothing.

We forgot everything
we knew on earth:
the words I and you,
mine and yours;
skin and caresses
and mothers' breast milk . . .
The Virgin Mary,
Mary Magdalene:
the highest, the lowest.
Now the two are one,
the trunk and the branch,
the first babe
of a new breed.

XXI. Stupid Thoughts On the Way Uphill

The best of all chimps
climbed down the trees,
leaving footprints in the sand
along the river banks.
Now man leaps
from rock to rock.

An angel of the Lord
came down then:
Drink from your mother's breast,

eta edan zazu ura.
Hau da biderik onena,
iraungitzeko gula.

Negu beltzeko gauetan,
ezta agertzen izarrik.
Porru gizenek iruntsi,
litzake edozein zerrik.
Horregatikan morroiak,
geratzen dira itzarrik.

Mundu guztiko lurretan,
gizona da nagusi.
Hura baino gauza bortitz,
edo sendoagorik.
Hegoitik iparraldera,
eztu lurrak ikusi.

Legeak debekatu du,
herrian geratzea.
Atzerritarren eskuan,
dirudi jungudeak.
Haur txikiaren odola,
edan duen sugea.

Kartagoko errautsetan,
etzen aurkitzen urik.
Hango amen ditietan,
eznea baitzen urri.
Haur txikiak hil ziraden,
gosez eta egarriz.

Hori da lege berria
Josepen ezpainetan.
Ta bere diru guztia,
doako limosnetan.
Ezta babarik egosten,
hemengo dupinetan.

Gauza guztien gainetik,
Jaungoikoa maitatu.

and then drink water.
That is the best way
to appease your hunger.

There are no stars
in the long winter nights.
Pigs could get fat
chomping down on leeks.
That's why night guards
don't sleep a wink.

Man is master
of earth's dominions.
No one is stronger,
more powerful, ever.
From South to North Pole
man rules the planet.

Laws forbid
remaining in the land
and our country rests
in other people's hands.
A snake drinking
the blood of a baby.

No water can be found
in the ashes of Carthage.
Little children died
of hunger, of thirst,
for no milk came forth
from their mothers' breasts.

That's the new law
from Joseph's own lips,
and all he owes he spends
spreading charity everywhere.
Bean stews no longer cook
in our pots old or new.

Love God
above all things,

Zure burua bezala,
lagun hurkoa amatu.
Orraziaren hortzekin,
zorririk ez zapaldu.

Eremuko arroketan,
armiarmak kantari.
Hare-arteko ziloan,
eztago denborarik.
Mendietako errekan,
urak daude gaur gazi.

Bide honetako amaian,
eztago mugarrkik.
Etxe erdi-erori hau,
munduan den guztirik.
Atzena da aurrerantzean,
eztago ezer bizkik.

Argizagiak astiro
debiltza izartegian.
Eguzkirik eztenean
iluminatzen dira.
Gauza misteriotsuak
gizonaren begian.

Antzinatikan gizona,
arrenoaren alde.
Gizonak bitinak hiltzen,
eta arranoak jaten.
Entzun ditugun pronuak
zan dira debalde.

and love others
as you love yourself.
Save the lice
from the comb's teeth.

The spider sings
among desert rocks,
and in the expanse of sand
time stands.
Mountain rivers
today run full of salt.

No rock marks
the end of this journey.
This crumbling house
is all there is.
Nothing lives, nothing dies,
what rests behind lies ahead.

Stars roll slowly
along the firmament,
When the sun goes out
they brighten up.
Big mysteries lurk
in human eyes.

Since ancient times
man and eagle side-by-side.
Man kills his victims,
eagle eats them up.
The screams
get nowhere.

ROCK & CORE

(Harri eta herri)

Couplets, Bertsoak, Sayings, and Poems

(Kopla, bertso, ditxo eta poemak)

LEHEN PARTEA

A): DOM PEILHENI HITZ APURTUAK

Hemen dago gizona. Paper
honetan dago. Nago.
Gizonago
sentitzen naiz.
Ta maiz
eznaiz
sentitzen.
Hortik dabil, eztakit
nundik;
agian
Lemoara doa tranbian.
Baina hemen,
paper honetan
dago.
Hemen imini du
bere zera. Zer da? Ezer ezta. Eder festa.
Esan zuen:

> *Jauna, berorren zerbitzari apur honek, jakin du nola etxe horretan libre dagoen giltzeroraren enplegoa. Beraz, nunbait teilatupe bat edukitzeko premia bizian aurkitzen naizelarik, atsegintasuna dadukat berorren Mesedeari nire zerbitzuak eskeintzean, eta*
> *eta eta eta . . .*
> *Jainkoak salba dezala Espainia.*
> *Halako egunean. Otxarkoagan*

FIRST PART

A): Broken Words for Dom Peilhen

Here is the man. He is
on this page. I am.
Here now
more of a man
something I don't
often feel.
He's out there, dunno
where;
maybe on a train to Lemoa.*
But here
he is
on this page.
He put himself here.
His self. What's that? It ain't. Let's dance.
He said:

> *Sir, this humble servant of yours has heard that your building is in need of a doorman. For this reason, and because I find myself without roof above my head, I hereby respectfully request to offer my services at your discretion, and*
>
> *and and and . . .*
> *May God save Spain.*
>
> *On such and such a day. In Otxarkoaga.**

Gizona apurra da.
Berak aitortu du.
Eta baldin hitz egin behar badut,
ezpanaiz isiltzen,
aire hitza
gizonaren parekoa izanen da, eta
        eta eta eta . . .
(noiz arte, Katilina!),
eta (lehen zen edo)
nire hitza zuri uzentzen dizudanean,
nire eskaratzetik hartzen dut ganibeta.
penaz eta ezin-bestean,
burnia sartzen dut haren barnean, eta entregatzen dizut
hitza
apurturik.
Gizonaren berdina izan dadin.
Hemen.
Jesus.

C): Souvenir d'Espagne pour mesdemoiselles solanje et Helena Gereziaga

Hau da Bilbo, esan zuen gizonak,
Kapela zuria zeraman gizonak, eta
Hau da Bilbo, esan zuen. *Hau da*
Pinturaren Museoa, esan zenuten.
Peut-être, esan nuen, *eztakit.*
Eznenkien ¿azer? Eznain lotsatzen.
Zergatik burjesa egonen da
museo honetan izenez, laudorioz,
(Halako konteak eman zen pintura hau),
pilotuaren eta marineruaren
izenak
hilobi baten gainean eztaudenean?
Zer da hori? Seinalatu zenuten leihotik.
Deustuko Eskola Jesuitena.
Ez, hangoa. Egurrezko etxe haek
Ijitoak, esan nuen lotsaturik.
Hurrutian entzuten zen trumoia.
Grekoa. Goia.

The man is humble.
He confessed as much.
And were I to speak,
and not remain silent
my word
would be equal to man, and
    and and and . . .
(how long, Katilina!)
and (before it was but)
when my word addresses you
I grab a knife from my kitchen
with sorrow, in despair
and drive metal into its belly
and give you
the word.
Broken.
So that it may be
equal to man.
So very.

C): SOUVENIR D'ESPAGNE POUR MESDEMOISELLES SOLANJE ET HELENA GEREZIAGA

This is Bilbao, said the man.
The man wore a white cap, and
Said: *this is Bilbao. This is*
the museum of painting, you two said.
Peut-êtré, I said, *I don't know*.
I didn't know. So what. I'm not ashamed.
Why are the bourgeois
in this museum, glory be,
(The Count of So and So donated this painting)
while the names
of the sailor, of the pilot,
don't grace their tombstones.
What's that? You pointed from the window.
Deusto University–Jesuits.*
Not that. Over there, the wooden houses.
Gypsies, I said, ashamed.
Thunder roared in the background.
El Greco. Goya.

D): Zorrotzako portuan aldarrika

Aleman barkua atrakatu da Zorrotzan.
Zimentua dakar, ehun kiloko sakoetan.
Bien bitartean
Anton eta Gilenzeuden
zerrarekin
tronko hura erdibitzen.
Sokarekin . . .
Eztago kablerik . . .
Bestela . . .
Tira eta tira,
Orain Anton,
gero Gilen,
eznaiz hiln,
Gilen.
Hemen euskeraz
ta han erderaz.
Birao egiten zuten,
okerbideak ezpaitaki mintzaerarik,
berdin tratatzen baitu
erdalduna
eta
euskalduna.
Arbolaren neurriak hartu nituen. Antiojuak bustitzen zitzaizkidan.
(Amak gauean pentsatu zuen errekara
erori nintzela). Eta esan nuen:*Beti paratuko naiz*
gizonaren alde.
Gilen.
Anton.

E): Hau izan da hasiera

Bai.
Eta egun batean isilduko naiz,
esan eztitudan hitzak esan ondoren.
Bai
Eta ez,
Beharririk duenak . . .

D): Swearing in the port of Zorrotza

A German ship has docked in Zorrotza.*
It's shipping cement, in 100-kilo bags.
Between them
Anton and Gilen were
sawing
a tree trunk in two.
With a rope . . .
we don't have a cable . . .
the other way around . . .
pull and pull,
now Anton,
now Gilen,
don't die then,
Gilen.
They swore.
In Basque here,
in Spanish there.
Because bad turns don't care about tongues,
they treat Basque
or Spanish
the same.
I measured the tree.
While my binoculars got drenched.
(That night mother thought I had
fallen in the river). And I said:
I will always be
on the side of men.
Gilen.
Anton.

E): This Was the Beginning

Yes.
And some day I'll shut up,
after I say
all the words I haven't said.
Yes
and no.
Let those who have ears . . .

F): ACT-I-18

. . . eta haren heste guztiak barraiatuak izan ziren luretik.

G): MIKEL LASARI AITA SAN FRANTZISKOREN BEZPERAN

Herenegun irakurri nion Oterori
zure poema Eganen agerturikako bat.

H): FORU SANTUAK DIO . . .

. . . Bizkaiko lurra
Bizkaitarrena dela.
Hala dio, Bladi.

I): BILBOKO ERDAL POETERIK TELEGRAMA

Bertan ezta sartzen eskribaurik,
ez apaizik,
ez zakurrik,
ez andredik,
Nork ematen du beste hainbeste?
Eta lastoa erretzen baldin badute
apezpikuaren joaeran,
nork eskeinduko du
beste hainbeste?

J): ENTZUN NAHI DIDANARI . . .

. . . esan behar diot eznagoela konforme . . . nire protesta presentatu behar dudala, gizonaren alde nagoela, behin Zorrotzako portuan prometitu nuen bezala. Nik eztut gauzarik asmatzen. Diodana egia da, eta eznaiz taktika zalea. Egia gurekin baldin badago, eztadukagu zergatik gezurrikan asma. Hala da, ni egiaren alde nago, gizona eta egia batera doazalako. Gizona egiatik aldaratzen denean, nik eztakit zer den. Eta inork entzen nahi ezpadit, berdin dit, esanen diot hiriari, izarrari, zeruari (oi hiri, oi izar, oi zeru), (seguru nago erantzutea kausituko dudala Getariar Mikel Lasa poeta berriaren alimoan), eznagoela konforme, nire protesta presentatu behar dudala, gizonaren alde nagoela. Esan dut. Nik eztut gauzarik asmatzen. Euskera Bilboko portuan ikasi dut, urdaiazpiko frijitua jaten nuenean, kafesne koinakatua edaten nuenean. Seguru nago gizona ere nire alde dagoela. Eta gizonak, agian, Mikel Lasa du izena. Batzutan pailasoz janzten da. Edo andreak Amaia Lasa. Ifar agirre.

F): Act-I-18

. . . and his bowels spilled over the ground.

G): To Mikel Lasa on Saint Francis's Vesper

Yesterday I read one of your poems
published in *Egan* to Otero.*

H): The Old Laws Say . . .

. . . that the soil of Bizkaia
belongs to the people of Bizkaia.
That's what it says, Blas.*

I): Telegram to the Castilian Poets of Bilbao

There is no room for the scribe here,
or for the priest,
or for the dog,
or for the woman.
Who offers as much?
And if they burn hay
always when bishops depart,
who is to give
quite as much?

J): To Those Who Will Hear Me . . .

. . . I must tell them that I don't agree . . . that I must make my protest clear, that I stand on the side of man, like I promised in the port of Zorrotza once. I never make anything up. What I say is the truth, and I am no strategist. If the truth is with us, there is no need to make up lies. It is so, I am on the side of truth, because man and truth are one. When man departs from truth, I don't know what he is. And if no one will hear me, I don't care, I'll speak to the city, to the stars, to the sky (oh city, oh stars, oh sky), (I'm sure I'll find answer in the heart of Mikel Lasa,* Getaria's new poet), that I don't agree, that I must make my protest clear, that I stand on the side of man. I've said it. I don't make anything up. I learned Basque in the port of Bilbao, while I ate fried cured ham, while I drank *café con leche* dosed with cognac. I'm sure too that man is on my side. And that man is called Mikel Lasa perhaps. He dresses as a clown sometimes. And the woman is Amaia Lasa.* North wind. Wind wind.

Haize agirre. Hegoi agirre. Munduko haize guztien agirrean, agirian. Euskal herria mundu agirre da.

K): Ni eta nik diodana

Ezer eznaiz, eznaiz ezer, ezpada
naizena.
Ni naiz naizena, bai, naizena, ez
eznaizena.
Ni naiz nirez,
nire borondatez,
naizenaren borondatez eta birtutez,
nire pentsamentuen eta sentimentuen indarrez.
Bidean nago (hain lege gogorra,
hain ordenamentu eskapu gabekoa),
bukaera batera. Hara noa eta
eznaiz bildurtzen, ez, eznaiz
bildurtzen, ez eznaiz
bildurtzen, ez,
Dena doa eztenaren bidean,
eta egun batean ezer ezta izanen, ezpada
ezer eztena. Ez. Bai. Ni naiz naizena,
eznaiz ezer ezpada
naizena, eta egun batean
ni ere eznaiz ezer izanen, ezpada
eznaizena, ez, izanen eznaizena.
Eta hau da, bai eta ez, orain eta beti eta lehen,
nik diodana,
eznaizena eta
isiltzen dudana.
Nire pentsamentuen graziaz eta birtutez.
Bai, Naizena. Diodana.

L): Nire izena

Hiltzen naizenean egonen da
nire lauzaren gainean eskribu hau:
Hemen datza Gabriel Aresti Segurola. Goian bego.
Perez y Lopez. Marmolistas. Derio.
Bizkaiko Bibliotekan ere egonen da
(deskomekatzen ezpanaute),
liburu bat (behar-bada, ezta seguru),

South wind. Open to the winds of the world, open wide, wide open. The Basque Country is wind is world is open.

K): I and What I Say

I am nothing, nothing I am, if not
what I am.
I am who I am, yes, who I am, not
what I'm not.
I am because of me,
because of my will,
by will and virtue of who I am,
by the power of my thoughts and feelings.
I am on the path (such harsh laws,
such inescapable demands),
headed toward the end. I'm going there and
I'm not afraid, no, I'm not
afraid, no I'm not
afraid, no.
Everything heads toward what isn't,
and one day there'll be nothing, only
everything that isn't. No. Yes. I am who I am,
I am nothing if not
who I am, and one day
I too shall be nothing, if not
who I'm not, no, who I won't be.
And this, yes and no, is now and always and before,
what I say,
who I'm not,
what I don't say
by grace and virtue of my thoughts.
Yes, who I am. What I say.

L): My Name

When I die
the following words will mark my tombstone:
Here lies Gabriel Aresti Segurola. Rest in peace.
Pérez and López. Marble masons. Derio.
And in the Bizkaia library
(unless they excommunicate me)
there will be a book (well maybe, I'm not sure)

inork letuko eztuena,
nire izenarekin. Eta
gizon batek esanen du kardanberak loratzen
direnean:
Nire aitak esaten zuen bezala, nik ere . . .
(Andre bat etorriko zait Done Santuru oro
lore koroa batekin).
Jainkoak eztezala nahi Bilboko karrika bati
nire izenik eman dezaiotela.
(Eztut nahi bizargile hordi batek esan dezala:
Ni'Arestin bizi naiz, anaiaren
koinata nagusiarekin. Badakizu. Maingua.)
Batzutan esan zaharrak erratzen dira.
Pentsatzen dut nire izena
nire izana dela,
eta eznaizela ezer ezpada
nire izena.

M): MUNDUAREN NEURRIA

Nire buruaz mintzatzen naiz, naizelako
munduaren neurria.
Barka bezaidate.
Nork bere begiekin ikusten ditu gauzak.
Eta nork diost niri Laudioko kanpandorreak
eztakusala? Nork?
Nire buruaz mintzatu behar dut, hura delako (ni naize-lako)
hobekien ezagutzen dudana.
Nire bularra labirintu bat da, dedalo bat,
eta bertako kale kantoi guztiak ezagutzen ditut:
Bertatik ibiliko naiz nola komodatik ohera,
arimaren begiak itsutzen dizkidaten egunean ere.
Dena dela, ni naiz mintzatzen naizena,
eta *mundua* diot,
nire zihorraz neurtu behar dut mundua,
beste neurririk ezin baitarabilket,
Nire bularraren gainean zer dagoen,
hori bakarrik jakin nahi dut.
Muntzatzen naiz nire buruaz.
Zarautzen gizon bat dago, gerra aurrean
egunero komekatzen zuena.

that no one will read,
with my name on it. And
a man will say, when thistles are in
bloom:
Like my father used to say, I too . . .
(And every All Saint's a woman
will visit with a wreath of flowers).
And please God, do not let them name
a street in Bilbao after me.
(I wouldn't like a drunken barber to say:
I live in Aresti, with my brother's
sister-in-law. You know. The lame one).
Sometimes old sayings are wrong.
I think my name
is what I am,
that without my name,
I am nothing.

M): The Measure of the World

I speak of myself because I am
the measure of the world.
Forgive me.
Everyone sees it their way.
Why attest that the church belfry
in Laudio* cannot see me? Who says?
I must speak of myself,
because I am
what I know best.
My chest is a labyrinth, a tangle,
and I know every nook, every cranny:
I can walk it as easily as my bedroom
even if my soul's eyes go blind.
Anyway, I am the one who speaks
and I say *world*,
and must measure the world with my stick:
what other measure can I use.
I only want to know
what rests on my chest.
I speak of myself.
There's a man in Zarautz* who before the war

Orain urtero bakarrik,
protestatu behar baita, ze demonio!
Hogei urteko alaba bat daduka,
pianoa, pintura eta alemana estudiatzen duena;
datorren urtean ezkonduko da, norekin eta
zubi injinero batekin!
Gizon horri etzaio gustatuko
nire buruaz mintza nadila, baina
hura ezta konturatzen ni naizela
mundu honetako gizonik jakintsuena.
Eztago jakitun, urrikaria.

took communion every day.
Now only once a year,
we must protest, what the hell!
He has a 20-year-old daughter,
she plays piano, paints, speaks German,
will marry next year -
nothing less than a civil engineer!
That man won't like
that I speak of myself, however,
he doesn't know that I am
the wisest man in the world.
Poor guy, he hasn't a damn clue.

BIGARREN PARTEA

A):

Beti esanen dut
egia.
Nire ahotik ezta hitzik aterako,
egia eztena.
Ezpainak apurtuko zaizkit,
hortzak eroriko zaizkit,
mihina ebakiko didate,
baina nik
eztut
gezurrik
esanen.
Eta inoiz,
nire juramentua hautsirik,
gezur bat badiot,
izanen da
eguzkia ilundu eztadin,
ilargia argitu dadin,
arrosak orriren bat irabaz dezan,
krabelinak. usainik gal eztezan,
haurra beti ditiaz goza dadin,
edo dontzeiliari
birjindadea joan dakion
nobleziaz.

SECOND PART

A):

I will always speak
the truth.
My mouth will utter no word
that is not true.
My lips will break,
my teeth will fall,
they'll cut out my tongue,
but I
will never
lie.
And if sometime,
I break my vow
and tell a lie
it will be
so that
the sun won't darken
the moon will shine
the rose grows a petal
the carnation holds its scent
the child takes the breast
and the dame
loses it
with someone good.

B):

Nire aitaren etxea
defendituko dut.
Otsoen kontra,
sikatearen kontra,
lukurreriaren kontra,
justiziaren kontra,
defenditu
eginen dut
nire aitaren etxea.
Galduko ditut
aziendak,
soloak,
pinudiak;
galduko ditut
korrituak,
errentak,
interesak,
baina nire aitaren etxea defendituko dut.
Harmak kenduko dizkidate,
eta eskuarekin defendituko dut
nire aitaren etxea;
eskuak ebakiko dizkidate,
eta besoarekin defendituko dut
nire aitaren etxea;
besorik gabe,
bularrik gabe
utziko naute,
eta arimarekin defendiuiko dut
nire aitaren etxea.
Ni hilen naiz,
nire arima galduko da,
nire askazia galduko da,
baina nire aitaren etxea
iraunen du
zutik.

B):

I'll defend
the family home;
from wolves,
from drought
from scammers
from justice
I'll defend
the family home.
I shall lose
the cows and sheep,
the gardens,
the pine forest;
I'll lose
the rent,
the interest,
the payouts,
but I'll defend the family home.
They'll take away my guns
and with my bare hands
and I'll defend
the family home;
they'll cut my hands off
and I'll defend
the family home
with my arms;
they'll leave me
without arms,
without shoulders,
without my chest,
and with my soul I'll defend
the family home.
I'll die,
I'll lose my soul,
my kin will stray,
but my father's house
will stand.

C):

Usoak dira,
eskribitzen dudanean
nire eskutik
ateratzen direnak,
poema hauk:

> Solanjeri Espainiako
> gomutaz
> eskeinirikakoak;
> Zorrotzako portuan
> asmaturikako
> protesta;
> Artxandaren aurrean
> kuzinatu nuen
> buzkantza.

Usoak dira,
kantatzen dudanean
nire ahotik
ateratzen direnak,
bertso hauk:

> Joaneren grazia
> eta bihotzak: bizkaitarreri
> emanikako
> esplikaerak;
> Australako kangurua
> eta Mikel
> Gezurra.

Uso hilak dira
eta bizi berri baten premian
daude.

D):

Ni naiz behin
esan nuena:

> Gu bizi garen munduan,
> gizarte honetan,

C):

They are doves
that,
when I write them,
fly out of my hands,
these poems:

> Those I wrote
> for Solange
> in memory of Spain;
> the protest
> I came up with
> in the port of Zorrotza;
> the blood sausage
> I cooked
> by Mount Artxanda.*

They are doves
that,
when I sing them,
fly out of my mouth,
these verses:

> Juan's grace
> and many hearts;
> the explanations
> to the people
> of Bizkaia;
> Australia's kangaroos
> and Mr Mikel's
> lies.

They are dead doves
in urgent need of life.

D):

It was I who
once said:

> In this world that we live in,
> in this society,

zuzenbidea
debekaturikan
dago.

Jainkoak ailiotsa
arnoa eta gazna
debeka
ezlezaten,
ura eta ogia
debeka
ezlezaten.
Gaur diot hau.
Bai. Nik.

E):

apur dezagun katea
kanta dezagun batea
hau da fandango
biba berango.

Munduan beste asko lez,
arta buruan oskolez.
Atzo aspertu nintzaden
maizuez eta eskolez.

Poeta naizen ezkero,
eztut zerurik espero.
Bederatzi kopa ditut,
lau zuhur eta bost ero.

Ilargiaren adarrak:
Handik zintzilik abarrak.
Gogoangarriak dira
zure bi begi nabarrak.

Zerutik dator harria.
Nundikan berriz argia?
Gau ilun honetan dakust
zure aurpegi garbia.

justice
is
forbidden.

Please God
don't let them forbid
wine
and cheese
don't let them forbid
water
and bread.
This I say today.
Yes. I.

E):

let's break the chain
let's sing as one
this is a fandango
*long live Berango**

Like many in this world
have done before with corn husks,
yesterday I got bored
with schools and masters.

Because I am a poet
I don't hold out for heaven
I've all of nine verses,
four good, five a bit cuckoo.

The horns of the moon:
adorned with dangly branches.
Unforgettable they are,
your kaleidoscopic eyes

The stone comes from the sky.
Where from, the light?
In this night so dark
your face is pure and bright.

Martxoko oilar gorria,
inundik ez etorria,
goseak arintzearren
judu batek igorria.

Goizaldean eguzkiak
printzak daduzka bustiak.
Oso merke saltzen dira
euskaldunaren ustiak.

Gure amonak esan dit:
Aitak arnoa edan dik.
joan zaitez tafernara
eta ekar zazu handik.

Euskeraren asturua
ezta gauza segurua:
Askozaz hobekiago
dabil munduan judua.

Eta hau hola ezpazan
ser nerila kalabazan.
Ipui txit barregarriak
kontatu nituen plazan.

F):

Maisu bat izan dut,
bakarra,
hori da nire errijent
gorena,
harengandik hartu nuen
eskola,
naizen euskalduna hari
zor diot,
aipatu behar dut haren
izena,
Gernikan bizi den
jaun hila,
Biarnoko plazan akabatu
zitzaigun,

Red cockerel of March,
came from nowhere,
a Jew brought it
to placate hunger.

At dawn the rays
of the sun look wet.
The opinions of Basques
sell like cheap trinkets.

Grandma told me:
Your dad's had too much drink
scamper to the bar
and bring him back right here.

The future of Euskara*
is by no means rosy.
Hebrew is far, far ahead,
its world pretty cozy.

Then pigs spoke rhyme
and monkeys chewed tobacco
and hens took snuff
and ducks went quack, quack, quack – oh!

F):

One
single teacher I've had,
my only my best
mentor,
he schooled me,
taught me,
I owe him
the Basque that I became,
I must mention
his name,
the dead man who lives
in Gernika,*
he who came to an end
in the square of Bearn,

hura paratu zen herriaren
aldean,
beraz etorri da nire
fabore,
gorputz hil bat
eztu neronen begiak
ikusi sekula
hainbeste urtetan
bizirik,
harek orain ni deskomekatu nau,
agian,
harekin nik komekatu dudalako
luzaro.
Altube maitea,
zure gorputz hila ezta inoiz hilen
berriz,
atzera,
neronen eskribuetan duzulako
bizia,
euskaldun herriak zaramazki
berekin,
zu biziko zara
betiko,
euskaldunen arimaren
barnean.

G):

Bi alaba ditut,
eta grinaren laguntzaz.
deseoaren laguntaz,
amodioaren laguntzaz,
etorriko zaizkidanak.

Andrea dut;
Jainkoak eman eta
Jondone Petrik
benedikatu zidana.

Etxe batek naduka
zor luze bati

he stood with the people,
that's why he is
with me,
a dead body
my eyes never saw
in so many years
alive,
he'll excommunicate me now
perhaps,
because I communicated
with him
for so long.
Dear Altube,*
your dead body won't ever die
again,
because your life
remains in my words,
the Basque people
carry you,
you'll live
forever
in our souls.

G):

I have two daughters,
and more who thanks to passion,
thanks to desire,
thanks to love,
shall come to me.

I have a wife,
who God gave to me,
and Saint Peter
blessed for me.

A house has me
tied to an endless

loturik,
hamar urte eta egun bateko
gartzela.

Bizia oso luzea da,
eta oraindik
are gehiago
prometitzen digute.
Mosu baten luzea
balitz,
ni
kontent
nengoke.

H):

Bigarrena izan zen
Joxepe Mikel
Ataungo.
Bigarren maisua,
bigarren zorra.
Gartzelatik ez ateratzeko
kondena
Joxepe Mikel maitea,
orain kontsola zaitea,
ezpaitzaude
bakarrik.
Joxepe Mikel haundia,
hamildu zaigu mendia,
orain posible da
eguna.

Orientean argitzen da
oilarite berri hori,
etorkizun bat eskeintzen
diguna.

J):

Esku beteka biltzen dut egia
aldamenean dauden gauzetatikan:
arrosa

debt,
jail for ten years
and a day.

Life is very long,
and they promise
there's still
more.
I'd be
happy
if it lasted
as long as a
kiss.

H):

The second was
Joxepe Mikel*
from Ataun.*
The second teacher,
the second debt.
Life
imprisonment.
Dear Joxepe Mikel,
console yourself,
you're not alone
anymore.
Great Joxepe Mikel,
the mountain crumbled,
daylight is possible
again.

Bright on the East already
the song of a new dawn
awakens
with another fate.

J):

I collect handfuls of truth
from everything I see:
the rose

eta haren bost orriak
krabelina
eta haren hamabiak:
eguneroko iratzartorduan
nire gelako leihoan
agertzen den
lehen eguzki printz iluna,
eta gaur eguerdian
Indautxuko plazan
neskatxa batek zuen
hulahupia.

Gizonen ahotik ez;
handik eztut egiarik biltzen.
Handik
iraina,
atzipea
eta enganamentua
dut biltzen.
Beraz,
gizonen ahoa tapatzen dut,
gauzak erakusten dizkiet,

hola
gizonaren semeagandik
ikus dezaten
posible dela oraindik
pizka bat
deskonponketa honi
nolabait
erremedioren bat
bilatzea.

K):

Inork badio:
Nire etxean eztago bakerik
bila beza
bakea
hauzoko etxean
edo munduko bazterrik

and its five petals
the carnation
and its twelve:
the first dark ray of sun
that alights
on my windowsill
daily as I rise,
and the hula-hoop
a girl played with
just today, at midday,
in Indautxu Square.*

But not from the mouths of men;
no truth to collect there.
There
I collect
grievances,
insults,
deception.
That's why I cover
the mouths of men
and show things instead,

so they'll see
from the son of man
that it is
still possible
just about
to somehow
find a solution
to this mess.

K):

If someone says:
there's no peace in my house
let them seek
peace
at their neighbor's
or in the remotest corner

azkenean;
baina etxean bakean balu,
eztezala gerrarik inun
bila,
bakea eta etxea
galduko baitu
munduko bazterretan.

L):

Munduan
gauza bat bakarra dago
erosten eztena:
Dirua.

M):

Ura darionean,
surik eztatxeka.

N):

Amaren oneriztea
alferrik galtzen da
oihalak batu artean:
Negarrak darama
eta azkenean
bederatzi hilabeteen oroitzapena
besterik
ezta geratzen.

O):

Jokoa ezta errenta,
esan zuen behinolako
Axularrek.
Ederki mintzatu zitzaien
aberatseri,
pobreok ezpaitugu
errentarik,
eta jokua gure
azken
esperantza

of the world;
but should they have peace at home,
don't let them seek war
elsewhere
because they're bound to lose
peace and home
in any corner of the world.

L):

In the world
only one thing
can't be bought:
money.

M):

When water flows
fire doesn't catch.

N):

A mother's regard
is lost in vain
among folds of fabric:
tears steal it
and in the end
only
the memory of nine months
remains.

O):

Old Axular* once said
that there's no annuity
in the hustle.
He spoke to the rich
very well,
because us poor
don't have annuities,
and the hustle
is our last
hope.

da.
Hola esan zidan
herriaren
ahoak.

P):

Axular
Gorbeia mendian
dago
ehortzirik.

Q):

Bilboko zimaurtegian
lore bat
aurkitu nuen.

R):

Amoriaren preziorik
merkeena
promesa bat da,
baina karioena
urrezko
eleztun
bat.

S):

Irrintzi gorri batekin
estaldun nituen
egunaren eta gauaren
ate meharrak.
Sega zorrotz batekin
ebaki nituen
pagadiaren
azken
lukurreriak
Teneza gogor batekin
atera nituen
debekazaleen
aginak.
Gero hil
nintzen.

That's what I heard
from the mouth
of the people.

P):

Axular
is
buried
in Mount Gorbea.*

Q):

In a landfill in Bilbao
I found
a flower.

R):

The cheapest price
of love
is a promise,
the most expensive
a golden
ring.

S):

With a red howl
I hid
the narrow doors
of night and day.
With a sharp scythe
I sliced
the old
usuries
off the beech tree.
With tough pliers
I tore the teeth off
the censors.
Then
I died.

T):

Argia
ezta
ikusten.

U):

Hobe
egia biribil bat,
ezen ez
mila gezur
ongi koadratu.

V):

Esanen dute
hau
poesia
eztela,
baina nik
esanen diet
poesia
mailu bat
dela.

W):

Egai bat esateagatik,
alabak
hil behar bazaizkit,
andrea
bortxatu behar badidate,
etxea
lurrarekin
berdindu behar bazait;
Egia bat esateagatik,
ebaki behar badidate
nik eskribitzen
dudan
eskua,
nik kantatzen
dudan

T):

You don't
see
light.

U):

Better
a round truth,
than
a thousand
squared lies.

V):

They may say
this
ain't poetry,
and I'll tell
them
poetry
is
a hammer.

W):

If, for telling a truth
they kill
my daughters,
they rape
my wife,
they flatten
my house;
if, for telling a truth
they slash
the hand
I use
to write,
the tongue
I use
to sing;

mihina;
Egia bat esateagatik,
nire izena
kenduko badute
euskal literaturaren
urrezko
orrietatik,
inoiz,
inola,
inun
eznaiz
isilduko.

X):

Egun batean
eztu inork
ezer erosiko;
egun batean
ezta merkatuetan
sagarrik
salduko.
Egun batean
guztiok
izanen gara
zoriontsuak.

Y):

Gauza bat dago
haltuetatik
Euskalerria
zaintzen
duena:
Axularren begia.

Z):

Joxepe,
nire laguna,
hurrun dago,
han goian,

if, for telling a truth
they erase
my name
from the golden
pages
of Basque literature . . .
even then,
never,
no way,
nowhere
will I ever
shut up.

X):

One day
no one
will buy anything;
one day
markets
won't sell
apples.
One day
we will
all be
happy.

Y):

There is this thing
that, from high above,
protects
the Basque
Country:
Axular's eye.

Z):

Joxepe,*
my friend,
is far away,
up there,

zerutik hurbil
eta ni berriz
hemen behean,
osin ilun honetan,
Bilbo deritzan
infernu honetan . . .
Hura han goian,
Arantzatzu deritzan
gailur haretan,
paradisu horetan . . .
Hemen
Baal,
Belial,
Lebiatan;
Bafomet,
Paladin,
Goteun,
Asmodeo
eta
Berzebu
dira
ene
lagunak,
baina
hura,
han
goian,
tobaritx
guztiak
baino
tobaritxagoa . . .

near the sky,
and I meanwhile
down here
in this dark well,
in this hell
called Bilbao . . .
He is up there,
on that peak,
in that paradise
called Arantzazu* . . .
Here
Baal,
Belial,
Leviathan,
Baphomet,
Paladin,
Goteun,
Asmodeus,
and
Beelzebub
are
my
friends,
but
he,
up there,
is comrade in-chief
of all
comrades.

IRUGARREN PARTEA

A):

Gauza zelaiak,
errezak
edonork konprenitzekoak,
esan behar ditut;
azalduko naiz
Bizkaiko
gizonik
tontoena,
baina hala ere
hatzamarra
eztit
inork
ahoan
sartuko.
listoa.

B):

Munduko gauza guztiak
gastatzen dira;
gastatzen da osasuna,
maitasuna,
deseoa,
bizioa;

THIRD PART

A):

Plain things,
simple ones,
easily understood,
that's what I must say;
I'll seem
the biggest fool
in Biscay,
nevertheless,
no one
is gonna shove
their finger
into my mouth.
They won't dare,
the smartasses.

B):

Everything in the world
diminishes;
health does, like
love,
desire,
vices,

guztizia,
bizia.
Eta errezen gastatzen da
munduko gauzarik iraunkorrena
gogorrena . . .
dirua . . .

C):

Siboneitik Kubanakanera
goajiro honek
egunero janen dut
nire arroz-aranke pizka,
egunero moldatuko dut
nire trokela,
egunero ikasiko dut
nire aleman
edo turko
lezioa,
egunero hartuko dut
nire katixima.
Egunero sentituko naiz
prestua.
Eta posible da
noizean behin
Ninarekin
ohean sartzeko
burjes
bekatua
kometi dezadala . . .

D):

Dirurik eztagoen egunean
ezta
gizonik
erosiko.

justice,
life.
And that which is most easily diminished
is the most perdurable thing in the world,
indestructible . . .
money . . .

C):

From Siboney to Cubanacán
this here *guajiro*
will eat a daily
serving of rice and herring,
every day I'll shape
my die cutter,
every day I'll learn
my Turkish,
my German
lesson,
every day I'll take
my catechism.
Every day I'll feel
honest.
And maybe one day
I might even commit
the bourgeois
sin
of bedding
Nina . . .

D):

The day there's no money
no man
will get sold.

E):

Axularrek
eman zion
Euskalerriari
itzala.

F):

Egun da Santi Mamina
Benetan egun samina
Goiko zeruan gorde dezala
Luzaro neure anima.

Esanen dizut egia
Hau ezta usategia
Erroi artean izan nintzaden
Benetan ausartegia.

Itsas aldean izarra
Hari begira lizarra
Euskera salbo ikusi arte
Eztut kenduko bizarra.

Kantatu zuen oilarrak
Argitzen dira belarrak
Agera gure martiriari
Moztu zizkaten bularrak.

Bularrak moztu zizkaten eta
Euskalerriak diotsa
Solomo luze dultzerik gabe
Eman zaidazu bihotza.

Eman zaidazu bihotza eta
Ken berriz nahigabeak
Esan noiz garen izanen gure
Etorkizunen jabeak.

E):

Axular
bequeathed
the Basque Country
his shadow.

F):

It's Saint Mammes* today
truly an ill-fated day
may Heaven keep my soul
for very, very long.

I'll tell you the truth
this ain't no pigeon loft
and among the crows
I've been braver than them all.

At the edge of the sea the star
and looking at her the ash
I tell you I won't shave
until I know Basque is safe.

The cockerel sang
the grass shone bright
and Agnes* our martyred saint
had her breasts sliced.

Had her breasts sliced
and the Basque lands demand
rather than your sweet loins
give us your heart.

Give us your heart
undo our sorrows
tell us if ever
our fate will rest in our hands.

G):

Kontuak eskatzen badizkidate,
esanen dut
eztakidala kontatzen,
oraindikan eztudala ikasi
bi ta bi
lau direla,
zeinbat diren
eskuan katzamarrak,
hamar ala hogei,
esanen dut
eznaizela
inoiz
kontuan erori,
eztakidala
gezurrik kontatzen,
eztakidala kontuz ibiltzen.
Baina halare
Begoñako herlojuan seiak direnean,
Urbiko zelaian,
begiak zabalik,
zortziko bat ezpainetan,
gizon on bat banintz bezala,
afusilatuko naute.

K):

Nik ere
badut
nire egia,
eta bankero jaunarenak
bezainbat
edo baino gehiago
balio du.

L):

Bilantzea koadratzen dut,
eta nire poesiak
kontrako partidarik ezpadu ere,
ikusten dut

G):

Should I be made to account
I'll say
I don't know how to count
I never learned
two plus two makes four,
how many fingers
in my hand,
ten or twenty,
I'll say
I never realized
I don't know
how to lie,
I don't know how to be careful.
And despite all that,
when the bells in Begoña* toll six,
on the plains of Mount Urbi,*
eyes opened clear,
a *zortziko** humming from my lips,
a quasi-honorable man,
I'll fall
under the firing squad.

K):

I too
have
my truth,
and it's worth
as much as
or more than
Mr Banker dude's.

L):

In tallying my balance
I see
that although my poetry
brings no returns

nola
datorren urterako
esperantzazko esistentzia haundi bat
dudan,
janarietako eta edarietako
prezioak
kariotzen badira ere,
egiak esateko negozio honi
malkarrotera joaten
utziko eztiona.

M):

Atzo ezagutu nuen
nire laguna.
Zerura pagatu nuen
kotxea.
Oñatin bazkaldurik
Arantzatzu gora,
bertan topatu nuen
fraile buru motza.
Atzo ezagutu nuen
nire laguna.

Arantzatzura bidea
benetan luzea,
hori menderatutzen
badaki kotxeak.
Zozoak eta
bildotsak dira
Andre dona Mariaren
lagunak.
Arantzatzu! Arantzatzu!
Polilitoa.
Joxepe lagun maitea:
Nun da zeruko atea?
Kanta dezagun batea!
Apur dezagun katea!
Begira nola dagoen
harana
hodei beltzez estaldurik, harantza

next year
I'll have a surplus of hope,
which,
even if the prices
of groceries go up,
won't bankrupt
this here business
of truth-telling.

M):

Yesterday I met
my friend.
I paid for a car
to Heaven.
After a meal in Oñati,*
up Mount Arantzazu,
I found a tonsured
friar.
Yesterday I met
my friend.

The road to Arantzazu
is truly a long one,
but the car
handles it.
The blackbirds
and the lamb
are Our Lady's
friends.
Arantzazu! Arantzazu!
Polylith.
Joxepe dear friend:
Where are Heaven's gates?
Let's sing all at once!
Let's break the chains!
Look, look at the valley
hidden
under black clouds,

nire deseoa haize hotzak
darama.
Hemen,
zozoen artean
bakea,
harmatu da bakea,
desarmatu dute
fedea.
Laguna,
aspalditik ezaguna.
Joxepe,
atzo ezagutu
zindudan
Zozoen txirulirua dator
agura,
Kolejiotikan dator
musika.
Nire bihotzean
tristura.
Noiz hartuko dut nik
alegria
berria?
Nork emanen dit niri?
Nor demoniok?
Goteunek ala
Belialek?
Aingeruen erreinuan
eztut nik ikusi
polilito bat
baizik.
Harria,
edonundikan
harria.
Harrizko dorrea.
Nundik etorria
izanen da
argia?
Nire fede
garbia?
Joxepe maitea,
esaidazu,

there my desire goes,
blown by the wind so cold.
Here,
among the blackbirds,
peace,
peace has been armed,
and faith,
disarmed.
My friend,
my long-time friend.
Joxepe,
I met you
yesterday.
The blackbirds tweet
rapid songs.
Music flows
from schools.
Sorrow in
my heart.
When will my time
for new joys
arrive?
Who will give it to me?
Who the hell?
Goteun?
Belial?
In the kingdom of angels
I've seen but one
Polylith.
Stone,
everywhere
stone.
Stone tower.
Where
did light
come from?
And my faith
so pure?
Dear Joxepe,
tell me,
promise me,

prometi zaidazu
egun batean,
etzidamu
edo zure edo nire
egunik azkenean,
esanen didazula,
arren,
nork dakarren
laugarren
bertutea.
Joxepe,
bai,
laugarren bertutea,
zerbaitean sinesteko,
zerbaitetik igurikitzeko,
zerbait maitatzeko
borondatea.
Borondatea:
Fede, esperantza eta
Karitatearen ostean
datorren
laugarren
bertutea.

N):

Egun batean
munduak akabatuko dira.
Bai.
Badakit.
Eta zerduko Jaunak
Josafateko zelaian
guztiok
juzgatuko gaitu.
Orduan,
Azkenak
izanen dira
lehenak,
eta haren eskuman
jarriko gara
ezkerrekoak.

that one day,
tomorrow or the next,
or on mine or your
last day,
you will tell me,
I beg,
who carries
the fourth
virtue.
Yes,
Joxepe,
the fourth virtue,
the will
to believe in something,
to hope for something,
to love something.
The will:
the fourth virtue
that comes after
faith, after hope
after charity.

N):

One day
all worlds will end.
Yes.
I know it.
And the Lord of Heaven
will judge us all
in the Valley of
Josaphat.
Then,
the last will be
first,
and on his right hand
we
the lefties
shall sit.

O): EUSKERA KLAROA

Lehengo egunean
esan zuen
nigatik
batek,
nire lagun oso maite batek,
eztakidala
zer dudan nahi,
baina bai
zer eztudan
nahi.
Hori egia da.
Baina egiagoa da
badakidala
zer dudan izan nahi,
baina
Kanako eztaietan
banengo
bezala,
esanen diot
nire amari
nire ordua eztela oraindik
allegatu.
Nire ordu hori
datorrenean,
alferrik izanen dira
damuak
eta nire arimaren kolorearen kontra
munduko
zezen eta aker ahari guztiak
oldartuko badira ere,
seinaleak izanen dira zeruan,
temploaren beloa urratuko da,
eguzkia itzalduko da,
mendiak zabalduko dira
eta lehen aldiz
andreak
erdituko dira
gizonez.

O): CLEAR BASQUE

The other day
someone said
about me
– he was a very dear friend –
that although
I don't know
what I want,
at least I know
what I don't
want.
That's true.
But truer still
is that I know
what I want to be,
but
like a guest of
the marriage at Cana,
I tell my mother
my time is
not yet nigh.
When my true time
arrives,
regrets
will be for naught.
And even though
all the bulls, rams, and billy goats
in the world
will plunge against the color of my soul,
there'll be signs in the skies,
the veil of the temple will tear,
the sun will hide,
the mountains will part,
and for once
women
will be born
of men.

Q): PROFETA BATI (JURGI OTEITZARI AZALDU NAHIRIK)

Behin batean gertatu zen,
eta ordutik aurrera
egunero gertatzen da,
gauza itsusi hau,
moldegaizki
hesteak apurtzen dizkiguna,
ezpairiogu onerizten gaiztakeriari,
higuintasunari ezpaitiogu amorerik emalten.
Halaxen da mundua,
eta gaur egunean
inor ezta profeta bere mendean.
Ilargiak zeruan
laranja gorri bat dirudi
mundu honetan isurden odolaren espilu.
Ilargian bizi bagintezke,
menturosoagoak izanen ginake.
Hea nork erregalatzen digun
marfilezko dorre bat,
eztezagun ikus
hemen gertatzen dena.
Nik eztut Jurgi Oteitza eskultorea ezagutzen,
baina hainbeste bider ikusi ditut haren harriak,
haren apostoluak,
bularretik egmikako baten ttua
edo gurdi batek zapaldurikako arratoiaren hilotza
balira bezala
kamino gaitz horretako bazterretan
eroririk,
ezen
oraindik eznaizen fariseoekin akort
geratzen;
harri hoek beren lekuan ikus ditzadan arte,
eztut errotarriekin
komekatuko.
Nire komunioa
haragizkoa eta edolezkoa
izanen da.
Hea noiz demonio, betetzen duten, bai,

Q) : TO A PROPHET (ATTEMPTING AN EXPLANATION TO JORGE OTEIZA)

It happened one day
and, since,
it's been happening every day,
this ugly thing,
which tears up our insides
in a bad way,
because we can't accept evil,
because we can't give room to hate.
That's what the world is like,
and these days
no one is a prophet in one's own century.
The moon in the sky
looks like a red orange
a mirror to all the blood spilled in this world.
We'd be happier
if we lived on the moon.
If only someone gave us
an ivory tower
to be blind
to what's going on here.
I don't know the sculptor Jorge Oteiza,*
but I've seen his stones so often,
his apostles
like sputum issued from a consumptive
or the flattened corpse of a run-over rat
abandoned
on the side
of this tricky road,
and I still
can't agree
with the Pharisees;
until I see those stones
where they belong,
I won't commune
with millstones.
My communion will be
of flesh
and blood.

harrizko aurpegi hori,
hortz-aginik gabe atso zahar baten begitarte zimela
baitirudi,
edo bestela
hiltzat emanik,
garizuma luze bat balitz bezala,
krubitxek more bat
jartzen dioten,
euskaldun kristauaren aurpegia
eztadin
lotsaz
mora.
Lehengo egunean aurkitu nintzen
nire pintore hura gabe;
eta honela Iparragirreren historia
geratu zen
bere pintura gabe.
Biharamunean nire musikalari zintzoa
aienatu zen
infernura edo
airerik eztagoen leku batera,
eta honela Iparragirreren historia
geratu zen
bere musika gabe.
Eztut sekula nik ikusi
haur bat
hain emazurtz
nola
nire Iparragirre
beraz,
Kantabriako itsasoaren kostaldera joan nintzen,
eta Izaroren aurrean negarrez,
nire poemaren urrezko orriak
entregatu nizkien
uhineri,
hobe baita itorik hil,
goseak baino.
Egunen batean Jurgi Oteitzarekin
otsaba bana txakolin gorri Arrankudiagako
edanen dugu,
eta orduan hura ere

Yeah, let's see when the hell they complete
that rock face,
that so far
looks like a toothless crone,
and if they won't,
give him up
for dead,
as if it were a long Lent,
dress him up
in a purple shroud,
and may the face
of Basque Christians
not bruise
with shame.
The other day
I found myself
without my painter;
and this is how Iparragirre's* story
found itself
without
its painting.
The following day my good musician friend
took a break
from hell I think,
or some other place without air,
and this is how Iparragire's story
found itself
without
a tune.
In my life
I have never known
a more orphaned
child
than my
Iparragirre;
this is why
I went to the Cantabrian Sea and cried
in the coast in front of the Isle of Izaro,
and offered the golden pages of my poem
to the waves,
because it's better to die drowning

kenduko didate,
eztadin inoiz munduan egon
poeta bat
ni bezain
bakarra.
Egunero Laudioko kanpandorrea ikusten dudanean,
fabriketako tximiniekin konparatzen dut,
eta ikusten dut
eztela hain gora,
diruak
fedeak baino
gorago
igotzen baitu.
Gure elizetako dorreek
haltuagoak izan behar dute,
eta zilo bat egin behar duku
aldare nagusitik
goiko gurutzera,
hea fariseoen otoitzek
zerura bide bat
bilatzen duten.
Orain Kaifas, ez bakarrik, tenploan,
gobernategian ere,
zutik dago.
Eztira oraindik konturatu
zerura
fariseoen fabriketako keek
igotzen dutela,
ez
haien otoitzek.
Batek ezan zidan lehengo batean
Aitaren belarriak gorrik daudela
hainbeste otoitz faltso entzutearekin.
Nik eztut holakorik sinesten,
baina emagaldueri eztiete dotrinarik irakatsi
eta publikanoek
gartzelaren kontrako hainbeste biro
eta hainbeste hitz zakar
esan dute,
ezen
oraingoz

than of hunger.
One day
with Jorge Oteiza
we shall drink a dram each
of red Txakoli* from Arrankudiaga
and then they'll take him
from me
too,
and then there won't be
another poet
like me
just as alone
in the whole wide world.
Every day when I see the bell tower in Laudio,
I compare it to factory chimneys
and see
that it's not as high
because money
reaches far higher
than faith.
Our church towers should be higher,
and we should drill a hole
from the main altar
to the cross above,
to see
if the Pharisees' prayers
find their way to heaven.
Now Caiaphas stands not only in the temple
but also
in the government palace.
They haven't realized yet
that smoke from the Pharisee's factories
is rising to
Heaven
and not
their prayers.
Someone told me the other day
that the ears of Our Father have grown deaf
from hearing so much false prayer.
I don't believe such things, but
they no longer teach whores the doctrine

mutu dauden.
Poetak bi klasetan berezi dira orain artean:
Prestuak eta doilorrak.
Orain artean, diot, bai, orain artean
prestuek egia esan dute beti,
eta doilorrek gezurra.
Baina orain egia esatea ezta naikoa,
orain arrazoia defenditu behar da,
eta orain harmak dira
gezurra eta egia.
Lehen arrazoia eta desarrazoia
harmak ziren
egiaren kontra edo fabore
edo
gezurraren.
Orain berriz egia eta gezurra
harmak dira
eztakit
arrazoiaren edo desarrazoiaren kontra edo fabore.
Lege zaharreko euskaldun prestu bati
inork esan balio inoiz,
euskaldun poeta batek
gezurrarekin defendituko zuela
arrazoia,
esanen zuen
lehenago apurtuko litzakeela munduaren ardatza
halakorik gertatu baino.
Holako egoera triste batera heldu gara, laguna.
Nik eztakit
Jurgi Oteitza defenditu bear dudan,
edo
Jurgi Oteitzak ni defenditu behar nauen,
ezpaitidate esan
nor den
bietatik
emazurtzago.
Egia da Oteitzaren eskultura eztudala
nik konprenitzen,
baina ni eskolarik gabeko gizon bat naiz,
eta hori ezta harritzekoa.
Baina Jurgi Oteitzak nire poesia konprenituko du,

and the publicans
have let forth so many blasphemies,
and said so many ugly words
that
they're dumb
now.
The poets have split into two classes:
the honest and the despicable.
Up until now, I say, yes, up until now,
the honest have always told the truth,
and the despicable, a lie.
But now it's not enough to tell the truth,
now reason must be defended,
and now the weapons are
lies and truth.
Before, reason and unreason
were weapons
for or against
truth
or
lies.
But now I don't know
whether
truth and lies
are weapons for or against reason or unreason.
If an honest Basque bound by the Old Laws*
had told someone
that a Basque poet
would defend reason
with lies,
he would have replied
that the earth's axis would crack
before he saw that.
But that's the sad state of things, my friend.
I don't know
whether I should defend Jorge Oteiza,
or,
if Jorge Oteiza should defend me,
because I haven't been told
who's the more orphaned
of us two.

dudarik gabe,
gauza errezagorik ezpaita inoiz
gizonaren eskutikan
atera.
Jurgi Oteitzaren eskultura konprenitzeko
bista luzearen behar da,
baina nire poesia konprenitzeko
ezta behar
belarri zorrotzen,
agian
harek listoentzat eskulpitzen zuelako,
eta nik
tontoentzat
eskribitzen
dudalako.
Nire poesia oso merkea da,
herriaren ahotik hartu nuen
debalde,
eta debalde ematen diot
herriaren belarriari.
Orian Jurgi Oteitza
eztakit nun
egonen den.
Ni hemen nago,
Basurtun.
Gaur kontuak atera ditut
eta etxera bihurturik ikusten dut
oraindik
telebista erosteko
eztudala
aski
irabazten.
Bista laburra dut, eta nire sudurraren aurrean dena
ikusten dut
bakarrik.
Zer egin behar dudan
inork esan dizaidan
nahi nuke.
Hainbeste atetan jo nuen nire
denporako egunetan,
hainbeste esku bilatu nuen adiskidetasun

Truth be told I don't understand
Oteiza's sculpture,
but I'm not a cultured man
so that's no surprise.
But Jorge Oteiza will understand my poetry,
no doubt about that,
because it's the easiest thing
to have come out of man's hand.
To understand Jorge Oteiza's sculpture
one needs far-sight,
but to understand my poetry
there's no need for far-ear,
perhaps
because he sculpted for the smart,
whereas
I write
for the fools.
My poetry is very cheap,
I got it for free
from the people's mouth,
and I give it back
for free
to the people's ear.
I don't know where
Jorge Oteiza may be.
I am here,
in Basurto.*
Today I did my sums
and once back home I see
I still
don't earn enough
to buy
a TV.
I'm short-sighted, and only see
what's right in front
of me.
I'd like someone
to tell me
what to do.
I called upon so many doors
in my day,

bila,
hainbeste andreren aurpegieri so egin nien
karino bila . . .
Baina orain eztago bihurrerarik.
Jurgi Oteitzak eztu jadanik
eskulpitzen,
bertsolariak
puntu aberatsen
eta
neurri gaitzen
etsai
deklaratu dira,
parlament-gizonek haien hautatzaileen kontra
diardukate . . .
Mundu honetan eznuke
bizi nahi.
Mila gezur esan behar ditut,
hea gizon prestuaren itxura
hartzen dudan:
Konparazio baterako:
Gizon onek andre onak maitatzen dituzte
edo
andre onek gizon onak errespetatzen dituzte,

> *Buskera klaro batean*
> *Oragin mintza gaitean*
> *Eznator derrigorrean*
> *Ezpada borondatean.*

Lehengo egunean esan zuen gizon zuhur batek
gizon zoroak ere behar diradela
mundu honetan.
Eztakit nola atrebitzen naizen
honela eskribitzera,
euskera klaro batean,
euskal garbi honetan.
Nik nahiago nuke,
egiaz diot,
holako bitz zakarrik
ez erabili,
ni ere garbi-zalea bainaiz,

I chased
friendship in so many hands,
I searched for love
on so many women's faces . . .
But there's no going back now.
Jorge Oteiza doesn't
sculpt anymore,
improvised verse singers*
have declared
their disdain
for the harder rhymes
and
the stranger schemes,
and parliamentarians
plot against their voters . . .
I'd rather
not live in this world.
I've to tell a million lies,
to look like I may be
an honest man:
For example:
Good men love good women
or
good women respect good men.

> *Let us now speak*
> *in a Basque that's neat.*
> *I'm not going to force anyone*
> *I just want a yes from everyone*

The other day a very wise man said
that this world
needs the crazies too.
I don't know why I dare
write like this,
in a Basque so clear,
in a Basque this neat.
I'd rather,
in truth,
not use such unworthy words,
because

hala esaten nion lehengo egunean
gure jakintsuari,
gure euskal berbo erromanizatu honetatik
erdal modu guztiak
sustraitik kendu,
nahiago nuke
iberiar eskrituran
eskribitu,
nahiago nioke
grekotik
nartu dugun
teknik hitz bakoitzari
euskal hitz egoki bat
kausitu,
eztadin honela
nirekin hasarra
inor,
eztezan inork
nigan
euskeraren kontrako gorrotorik
bila . . .
Baina hola gertatu da,
eta nik eztut kulparik.
Mundu guztiaren kontra
nola ausartuko nintzake?
Nire lekua dago
herriaren aldean.
Nirekin dagoena
Euskal Herriarekin dago,
ni harekin bainago.
Udarregi bertsolariak
etzekien erderaz
mintzatzen,
baina hala ere
erdera asko zekien.
Hemen, Laudion, bizi den gizon horrek
eztu sekula konpremtuko
ze dieferentzia haundia ematen dion
gure aberriaren bizitza propioari
Z jostagarri horrek.
Basarrik berriz erderaz daki

I'm a purist too,
that's what I said the other day
to my very wise friend,
that I'd rather tear all foreign forms
off these our Romanized Basque verbs,
that I'd rather use
Iberian script,
that
I'd rather find
one good Basque word
for every technical word
we've taken from Greek,
so that
no one
is upset
with me,
so that
no one
accuses me
of hating Basque . . .
But this is how things are,
and it's not my fault.
How can I fight
the whole world?
My place is
with the people.
Those who are with me
are with the Basque Country,
because I am with it.
Udarregi* the verse singer
didn't speak Spanish,
but despite that
he knew a lot of Spanish.
This man who lives here in Laudio
will never understand
the difference it makes
to the very life of our homeland
to have all those playful Zs.
But Basarri,* on the other hand,
speaks Spanish
perfectly,

ederki,
nik beste;
Baina bala ere eztu
erderarikan batere
ikasi.
Orain ikasi
behar dut
erdera.
Baina holako gauza gaitzik ikasitzeko,
eztu oraindik inork libururik
eskribitu,
eta honela
nire aprendiz-aroak
luzaro
iraunen du.
Orain galdera bat egin nahi diot
eztakit nori:
Zergatik rnetitu ote naiz
halako enplego txar batean?
Zergatik sartu ote nituen
sudurrak
hain kirats txarreko
zer-egin honetan?
Baina zergatik?
Ez nintzen ni ederki bizi
Bilboko hirian,
gaztelaniaz,
hispanidadean?
Baina ez.
Nire leinuaren ezagugarria da.
Ur lasterraren kontra iher egiten dugu.
Baina hau nola ulertuko da?
Nola adituko da?
Herriaren karruzelean dantzan egiten badut,
nola izanen naiz otso bakarti bat?
Kaietako tafernetan arno beltza edanen badut
aleman ontziari planto egin dioten langileekin,
nola hartuko dut
eremutarren
antzik?
Baina hau erraxki konprenituko du Jurgi Oteitzak

as well as me;
but despite that,
he hasn't learned anything
in Spanish.
Now I have
to start to learn Spanish.
But no one has ever written
a book
to learn such a difficult thing,
and for this
my apprenticeship
is bound
to take long.
Now I want to ask a question
to I-don't-know-who.
Why did I enter
such a bad profession?
Why did I dig my nose
into such foul-smelling
business?
But why?
Didn't I live happily
in the city of Bilbao,
in Spanish,
in the Hispanic world?
But no.
It's a mark of my lineage.
We must swim against the current.
But, how will this be understood?
How will they comprehend it?
If I dance in the people's carrousel,
how can I hope to be a lone wolf?
If I must drink red wine in port bars
with the stevedores that said fuck you to German ships,
how can I hope
to look
like a hermit?
But this Jorge Oteiza will easily understand
just as
Gabriel Zelaia* and Agustin Ibarrola*
have,

Gabriel Zelaiak eta Augustin Ibarrolak ere
konprenitu duten
bezala,
nire lagun gustiek,
nik ezagutu bai eta eztitudanek
konprenitu edo
konprenituko duten bezala.
Nire burruka, hala ere,
haundiagoa da.
Nire lagunen etsaiak
adimentutsuak dira;
nireak berriz, adimenturik
gabekoak.
Jainkoak libra gaitzala,
esan zuen Bladik,
neskatxa itsusietatik.
Nik diot:
Deabruak gaitzala libra
agure eroetatik.
Bilbon agure ero bat dago,
zenaren izenaz akordatu ere
eztudan nahi.
Jesukristok berak ere etzuen ukan
etsai traketsagorik.
Aireari eta Arenaleko astigarrari
galdetuko nieke
zer deabru edo zer aingeru
egin diodan nik
gizon horri.
Nire aurpegia etzaio gustatuko?
Baina espiluan begiratzen diot ene buruari,
eta ikusten dut
nire begitarteak
eztirela
itsusiak.
Egia da antiojuak erabiltzen ditudala
eta ezpainaren gainean
eztadukadala
biboterikan,
baina hala ere
edozein andrek

like all my friends will understand,
those I have met and
those I have yet to meet.
But despite that my fight
is bigger than that.
My friends' enemies
are clever,
not, alas,
mine.
May God save us,
said Blas once,
from the ugly ones.
And I say:
May the devil save us
from stupid old men.
There's a stupid old man in Bilbao
whose name
I don't care to recall.
Not even Christ himself
had a more twisted foe.
I'd like to ask
the air and the linden tree in the Arenal*
what the hell
or what the heavens
have I done to that man.
Maybe he doesn't like my face?
But if I look in the mirror,
I see
my features
are not
that bad.
It is true that I wear glasses
and I don't have
a moustache,
but besides that
any woman
would say
I'm quite the catch.
This never happens though
because money is too expensive
to buy.

hartuko ninduke
galaitzat
Holakorik ezta gertatzen,
dirua kario erosten delako
mundu honetan.
Baina nire bizitzaren historia kontatzen
ausartuko banintz,
inork ezninduke aurkituko
hain higuingarri.
Baina ahal balu
agure ero horrek
bizien arteko listatik
borratuko ninduke.
Zorriak oso
aspergarriak
dira.
Koreako gerran naikos nahigabe
eman zidaten.
Baina orain,
baketean,
hainbeste dutxa egonik,
eztakit
nola sortzen diren.
Nik eztut sinesten
lurra mintza dakiola
inori,
baina hala ere
gizon oso prestu batek esan zidan lehengo egunean
Jurgi Oteitzak,
Aita Donostiaren oroitarria imajinatu baino lehen,
kromeleketako lurrarekin
egin zuela
hitz,
lurrean geratzen baitira
ez bakarrik gizonen eta andreen hezurrak,
baita haien pentsamentuak eta sentimentuak ere
baizik.
Jurgi Oteitzak
lurrareldn hitz egin zuen;
nik eztut holakorik sinesten,
baina hala ere

And if I dared tell the story
of my life,
they wouldn't think me
so hateful.
And if he could
that stupid old man
would erase me
from the list of the living.
Lice
are
unbearable.
During the Korea War
they wouldn't let me live.
And now,
in times of peace,
with such abundant showering
I don't get
their plenitude.
I don't believe
the earth speaks
to anyone,
but despite that
the other day a very honest man told me
that Jorge Oteiza
before imagining the monument to Aita Donostia*
spoke
to the soil
to the cromlechs,
because it's not only the bones of men and women
that rest in the soil
it's also
their thoughts and feelings.
Jorge Oteiza
spoke
to the rocks;
I don't believe such things,
yet
I know them
to be true.
Because Jorge Oteiza is not a man,
because Jorge Oteiza is a superman;

egia dela
dakit.
Jurgi Oteitza ezpaita gizon bat,
Jurgi Oteitza gizonago bat baita;
azken bolada honetan pentsamentura ekarri naute
hura
profeta bat
dela.
Antigoalean
profetak
harrika
hiltzen zituzten.
Gaur egunean
arbuioz,
desamodioz
eta
desprezioz.
Nik eztakit nola Jurgi Oteitzak
agoantatu duen
orain artean
hainbeste
desprezio
Bilboko zorriak
Euskalerri guztira
sakabanatu dira.
Horrelako izurterik ezta ikusi
Europan
Edade Ilunetik;
bakarrik
aurkituko da
konparazioa
Enperadoreen Aldiko
Sinan
edo
behin sakratuen
Hindia pobreegitu horretan.
Zorriak abaro bila doaz, ez bakarrik
soldadoen eta garbitzaleen semeen boruetara,
orain Akademietan
eta Apezpikutegietan
aurkitu dute

and lately my thoughts have told me
that he
is
a prophet.
In the old days
they stoned
prophets
to death.
Nowadays,
they're neglected,
unloved,
ostracized.
I don't know how Jorge Oteiza
withstood
so much
disregard.
Bilbao's lice
have spread
to the entire Basque lands.
Such a plague we've not seen the like
in Europe
since the Dark Ages.
This is only comparable
to China
in the time
of the Emperors
or
to impoverished India
with the sacred cows.
Lice seek shelter not only
in the heads of street sweepers and soldiers,
now they find
the protection
of Royal Academies
and Bishops' Palaces.
They retire,
like normal people;
they say:
his hands (or his soul, they don't care)
are tainted with blood.
And in this way

babesa;
persona normalak balira bezala
jubilatu egiten dira;
diote:
Horren eskuak (edo arima, berdin baitie),
gorriz tintaturik daude.
Eta honela deskomekatzen dituzte
Parnasotik
poetak,
eskultoreak
edo pintoreak;
elizatik
etxeko jaun prestuak;
fabrikatik
langile trebeenak.
Edo deskomekatzen ezpadituzte,
asper-arazitzen diete,
eta azkenean
dimisioa presenta-arazitzen diete
motiborik apurrenarekin.
Nik poetatzatik
dimisioa
presentatu nuen
kantsazioaren aitzakiarekin.
Baina nola aitzakia hura gezurrezkoa zen,
berriz ere artu nuen eskuan mailua,
eta Kantabriako itsasoa jo dut golpeka.
Jurgi Oteitzak ere
kromlekaren aitzakiarekin
dimisioa presentatu zuen
eskultoretzatik,
baina hala ere
inork eztio Euskalerriari
penamenik eman.
Euskaltzaleak ezkara lutoz
beztitu
Tente jarraitzen dugu,
jakin gabe
munduan behin eskultore bat egon zela
Jurgi Oteitzaren izenarekin.
Nik eztakit Jurgi Oteitzak zer esanen duen

they banish
from Parnassus
the poets
the sculptors
or
the painters;
from church
the most honest *pater familias*;
from the factory
the most gifted workers.
If they don't banish them,
they bore them to death
until, in the end,
they are made to quit
for the flimsiest reasons.
I too
resigned
from poetry
alleging tiredness,
but since my pretext was false,
I held my hammer high again
to bang against the Cantabrian Sea.
Jorge Oteiza
with the pretext of the cromlechs
resigned from sculpture
too,
but no one is sorry for his loss.
The Basquephiles didn't dress
for mourning.
We carry on
without the knowledge
that there once was a sculptor
called Jorge Oteiza.
I don't know what Jorge Oteiza will say
when he reads these verse-statements,
he may think
I'm not right in the head
(it's true I don't want a *txapela* beret or a crown of laurels),
he may
say
that in Bilbao we don't make

poesi-punto hauk irakur ditzanean.
Behar-bada esanen du
nik eztudala bururik,
(egia de eztudala txapelik edo ereinotz-koroarik irabazi nahi),
esanen du,
naski,
Bilbon eztagoela sobera kanorerik,
sobera zentzurik,
eta honekin erakutsiko dit
nola
profetak ere
zorritasunez
kutsa litezkeen.
Baina nik azaldu behar diot,
esplikatuko diot,
zer den,
zergatik bera oraindikan ezten
euskal arimaren zolara heldu,
gu itotzen garen
infernu behere honetara.
Gu ezkara hemen lasai bizi.
Guk eztugu zentitzen
paradisu bat.
Dantek ere etzuen holakorik
asmatuko.
Hau da basatza haundi bat.
Hemen aingeruen arimak ere likistuko lirake.
Hemen bakarrik gordetzen dira garbirik
dontzeila aberatsen florea,
ezen ez lorea.
Hemen ezin liteke haruagarik har
Hemen ito egiten da libertatea.
Gizonak erosten dira,
sagarrak bezala,
andreak saltzen dira
madariak bezala.
Hemen orok du bere prezioa:
Eskeinduera eta eskatueraren erreinua da hau.
Hemen Jurgi Oteitzaren eskulturak ere,
Agustin Ibarrolaren pinturak ere,
Gabriel Zelaiaren poesiak ere,

much sense,
that we're not
very capable,
and with that he'll demonstrate
that
prophets
unfortunately
can also
catch lice.
But I have to explain
I have to make him understand
what is what
and why he still hasn't understood
the truth of the Basque soul,
this lower hell
where we drown.
We don't live happily
here.
This isn't paradise
for us.
Not even Dante could have come up
with this.
This is a big mud bath.
Even the souls of angels would get mucky here.
The only purity preserved here
is the flora of rich damsels,
not so much their flower.
It's impossible to breathe here.
Liberty gets choked here.
Men are bought,
like apples,
women are sold,
like pears.
Everything has a price here:
This is the kingdom of supply and demand.
Here even the sculpture of Jorge Oteiza,
even the paintings of Agustin Ibarrola,
even the poetry of Gabriel Zelaia,
are bought and sold.
Here there's only one thing
no one buys or sells,

saldu eta erosi egiten dira.
Hemen bakarrik gauza bat dago
inork saltzen edo erosten eztuena
eta hori da
Gabriel Arestiren poesia,
hain merkea baita
ezen eztuen preziorikan.
Nik eztiot
botako
hemen gertatzen denaren kulpa
inori;
Madrilen eta Parisen ere
aingeruxka inuzentak dira,
eta Bilboko eta Donostiako kapitalisten gainean ere
eznaiz ausartuko,
haien arimetan
ezpaiomendago
Adamen bekatutik
arrastorik ere.
Hemen oro da garbitasuna,
Iangileek andreek
beren gizonen izerdiak
kentzen baitituzte
banko-etxeetako patioetatikan.
Egunkari katolikoak ere egiaztiak dira.
Hemen eztu inork gezurrikan esaten.
Hemen oro da zilegi,
baita euzkotar abertzaleen erotasuna ere.
Hemen inor ezta konturatzen
ekaitz haundia
hurbil
dagoela . . .
Baina nola esplikatuko diot nik
hau
Jurgi Oteitzari,
nola sartuko diot Gabriel Zelaiari
nik hau
buruan,
nola ausartuko nintzake ni
Agustin Ibarrolari
honen gainean

and that's Gabriel Aresti's poetry,
because
it's so cheap
it can't be bought.
I won't
blame
anyone
for what's going on here.
Even in Madrid and Paris
they're little innocent angels,
and I don't have the guts
to go against Bilbao or Donostia's* corporate lords,
because there is no trace
of Adam's sin
in their souls.
Here everything
is pure,
worker's wives
pat their men's sweat
dry
from the bank's courtyards.
Even Catholic newspapers tell the truth.
Here no one lies.
Here everything goes,
including the madness of Basque nationalists.
Here no one realizes
that the big storm
is near . . .
But how can I explain
this
to Jorge Oteiza,
how can I get
this
into Gabriel Zelaia's
head?
How can I dare
to speak
to Agustin Ibarrola
about this,
when they
are wiser

mintzatzen,
ni baino jakintsuagoak
baldin
badira?
Inork eztu
nik baino
adimenturik gutxiago.
Gabriel,
nun dago
kanorea,
nun daukazu
zentzua?
Gabriel Aresti Segurola,
mutil gaisoa,
zergatik atrebitu zinen
itsaso honetan,
enplego txar batean
zinaden metitu,
horregatik etzinen
hemen ametitu.
Oterori diotsat:
Que tal Hikmet y tu?
Konta zaidazu bada . . .
Baina hau ezta zortziko txikiaren ordua.
Hemen gertatzen dena
kontatu behar dut.
Zortziko nagusian
kantatu behar dut.
Gure Euskalerria
sendatu behar dut.
Arrisku honetatik . . .
Baina hau ezta bertsolarien eguna.
Lehengo egunean egon nintzen
Gernikako frontoian.
Lehioak
ikusirik han
goian,
pentsatzen dut gure gauza
galdu zela sasoian.
Bart entzun nion bati
euskal kuzinaren gainean mintzatzen,

than me?
No one
understands
less than I do.
Gabriel,
where is
your acumen,
where did you
leave your senses?
Gabriel Aresti Segurola,
unfortunate boy,
why did you brave
these seas,
why did you enter
this losing business?
That's why
you'll never belong.
I said to Otero:
How are *Hikmet y tú* . . . ?
Go on, tell me . . .
But this isn't the time for a minor *zortziko* tune:
I must say
what's happening here.
And I must sing it
in a major *zortziko* tune.
I must make
our Basque land heal.
From this great risk . . .
Even though this isn't the improvised verse singers'
Bertsolari Day.*
The other day I went
to the *fronton* court in Gernika.
Seeing
the windows
high above,
I thought our thing
got lost on time.
Last night I heard someone
talk about Basque cuisine,
and how eggs should be cooked
below the stove.

nola arraultzak jarri behar diren
sukaldearen azpian.
Nire gainean zerua,
nire azpian lurra . . .
Nire gainean eztute hitzik egiten,
baina kentzen dute hautsa
nire azpitik,
inuntzi batekin.
Eta orain Jurgi Oteitzari esan behar diot egia:
Errusinolaren kantuak
nire arima
bakez
betetzen du.
Hura entzuten dudanean
melodia atsegin bat
sortutzen zait
barnean.
Errusinolaren kantuak
gogora ekarten dit
nire amaren sabelean
gozatzen nuen
naretasuna.
Itsasoaren uhinetan
enbarkatuko banintz,
eznintzake
mundu ederrago batetik
nabegatuko
inola.
Nazareteko Jesus
etzen nabegatu
bederatzi hilabete haietan
kontentago.
Mundua ederra da,
errusinolaren kantua baino
ederragoa;
Nerbioneko hibarrean
udazkeneko arratsetan
pinudiek
arimari ematen diote
mosutxu luze bat;
negar egin nahi balukete bezala

The sky, above,
the earth, below . . .
They're not talking about me,
but they're sweeping the dust
below me
with a broom.
And now I must tell Jorge Oteiza the truth:
The nightingale's song
Fills me
with peace
to my core.
When I listen to it
a beautiful melody
is born inside of me.
The nightingale's song
floods my mind
with the stillness
I enjoyed
in my mother's womb.
Navigating
the sea's waves,
wouldn't make
the world
more beautiful to sail.
Jesus of Nazareth's own
nine month's travesy
was no happier
or better.
The world is beautiful,
more beautiful than the nightingale's song.
In the valley of Nerbion,*
at dusk, in the fall,
the pine forests
lock my soul
in a long kiss;
as if they were about to cry
they flood
with bright obscurity,
like a mirror
held to my eldest daughter's face
when

iluntasun argi batez
betetzen dira,
badirudi nire alaba nagusiaren aurpegia
kopiatzen dutela,
hari
Nerea,
deiadar egiten diodanean,
tristeziaz betetzen baita,
eta
Guria izan da,
ihardesten badit,
eta gero
Etor hadi honera,
esaten diodanean,
hik eztun ezer egin,
eta hire inuzentziaren errua
eztadukan zergatik
hire ahizparen gainean
bota,
haurtxoari alaitasuna baitatorkio
begitartera.
Horrelakoa da gure lur maitea
Nerbion hibaiaren ondoan,
udaren eta neguaren arteko egun nabarretan,
gau iluna hurbiltzen zaigunean,
ilunabarra
erori baino lehen.
Nik eztakit, bada, zer dudan, ez, maiteago,
gure lurra
edo
nire alabak.
Haek dira niretzat
lurreko gatza,
itsasoko usaia
eta aireko soinua.
Errusinolaren kantua motza da
haiekin konparaturik.
Nire alabekin baldin banoa
espiritutsuagoa da arno zuria,
zaporetsuagoa muskuilua
eta urrintsuagoa Birginiako orria.

I shout
Nerea,
and she fills with sadness,
and answers
it was Guria,
and later
when I tell her
come here,
you haven't done anything
there is no need
to blame
your innocence
on your sister
and her child's eyes
fill with joy.
That's what our soil
on the shores of the Nerbion
is like
on those limpid days between fall and winter,
when the dark night inches close
just before
dusk.
So I don't know what I love the more,
our soil
or
my daughters.
For me, they are
the salt of the soil,
the scent of the sea
the melody of the air.
The nightingale's song doesn't begin
to compare.
When I'm with my daughters
white wine brims with spirit,
mussels are the tastiest
and
Virginia leaf so aromatic.
The light
is brighter,
the air
is breezier,

Argia
argiagoa da,
haizea epelagoa,
eta uliinak
ederragoak.
Argia da egun oso luze bat,
haizea da igurikiera atsegin bat,
uhinak dira gizonaren gogoak deseaturikako gutiziak.
Nire adiskideak dira.
Mundakako elizondoan jezartzen naizenean,
nire begiak Izarori erregalatzen dizkiot
eta haiekin mintzatzen naiz luzaro.
Egun batean bertan nengoelarik,
kopla bat kantatu nion:

Hor zaude apal Izaro
Hementxe harro Lazaro
Bizitza berri honetan iraun
Azi nezazu luzaro.

Baina damutu nintzen,
gure mintzabideak ezpaitu lekurik hartzen
hitzetan,
hobe baita
mutu geratu,
ezen ez hitzetako pisu traketsarekin
adiskidetasuna
trabatu
eta zikindu.
Asko maitatzen dut
Kantabriako itsasoa,
nire lagunen presentzia
eskeintzen baitit.
Baina bertan nagoenean
Nerbioneko hibar goikoa
etortzen zait gogora,
eta orduan Bizkaia arineketan igaratzen dut.
Arrigorriagatik gora igotzen dut,
eta pinudien presentziaren aurrean
nire lagunen ausentzia
damu dut.

the waves
more beautiful.
Light is a very long day,
air a pleasant waiting game,
waves are the wishes of men.
They are my friends.
When I sit by the church in Mundaka*
I offer my eyes to the Isle of Izaro
and talk on and on.
One day while sitting there
I sang them this song:

> *There you are sweet Izaro*
> *And here proud Lazaro*
> *Grant me a long hold*
> *of this new lifeblood.*

But I regretted it,
because our conversations don't take place
in words,
because it's better
to be quiet
than to hamper
and pollute
friendship
with the burdensome weight of words.
I love the Cantabrian Sea
so much,
because it brings me
the presence of my friends.
And when I'm there
I remember
the steep valley
of the Nerbion River,
and then I run across Bizkaia,
I float above Arrigorriaga,*
and feel the pain
of my friends' absence
in the presence of the forests.

LAUGARREN PARTEA

A): Astepeko sekretarioren bertso berriak

Iparragirren bozian nuan
bertso batzuk esatera
Lege zarrian zergatik jarrai
arrazoia ematera
    Ni eznauzu atera
    Inoiz plaza batera
Bertsolarien moldian
Zoritxarrian ez det ikasi
solo artian goldian.

Euskalerrian ez det ikusi
oraindik bide zuzenik
Orregatikan ez det egingo
aipatu nire izenik
    Inoiz ez det esan nik
    Kaletarra naizanik
Edo-ta baserritarra
Iparragirrek bezala egun
joko det nire kitarra.

Sarri askotan deitu dirate
niri bizkaitar iskua
Baina Bizkaian jaio ez banaiz
ez da miragarrizkua

FOURTH PART

A): New Verses by Astepe's Secretary

I am now about to sing
a few verses like Iparragirre did,
to justify the need
to trust the Old Laws.
  I've never been asked
  to sing in the square
like our verse singers do.
Likewise unfortunately for you
lifting rocks* is not something that I do.

So far in the Basque lands
I've seen not one straight path,
given all that
I won't say who I am
  I've never revealed
  whether I'm a farmhand
or if instead I'm kinda urban.
Like Iparragirre in his time
I'll just go and play guitar.

I've often been called
the Bizkaian stud.
Since I wasn't born in Bizkaia
isn't that sort of miraculous?

Ni ez naiz arrizkua
Bai ori arriskua
Danok aurkitzen gerana
Beraz sekula ez da jakingo
gaur eskutatzen derana.

Tratantiaren moduan nago
Gipuzkuan ibilia
Gauza geiegi jakina dago
erdaldun euskaltzalia
Ni naiz animalia
Eros ta saltzalia
Beti prezio merkian
Orregatikan ez naiz bizitzen
aberatsen subertian.

Aberastutzen ez dan gizona
ori da gizon prestua
Bere lagunen ondasunera
ez duakio eskua
Au ez da legezkua
Ez arrazoiezkua
Zergatik degun ikusten
Nola andiak txikiakatik
poltsak betetzen dituzten.

Mundu onetan justiziarik
es da sekula ikusi
Juez jaunaren ofiziua
ori da gauza itsusi
Tranpak dira nagusi
Legia dute ausi
Bein deklaratu zutenak
Premiatuak izango dira
erruz lapurtzen dutenak.

Nire erriko alkate jauna
eta apaiza dirade
Gure baserri aberats batez
dirurik pagatu gabe
Ederki egin jabe

I'm no rock
that'd be dangerous
not just for me but for all of us.
So shush now and let me keep
my secret where it is.

I've crisscrossed Gipuzkoa*
in my work as a cattle dealer
and as a Basquephile Spanish-speaker
I now know much too much
I sell animals
I buy animals
always very cheap
that's why I don't live
anything like the rich.

The man who doesn't get rich
that's a good, solid man
someone who won't grab
for his friend's bag.
That's not legit
nor the way it should be.
Yet we keep seeing this,
the big fish filling their pockets
with the wee.

In this world justice
is a big unknown
the job of Mr Judge
so ugly you could choke
cheaters reign
laws are broken
by those meant to promote them.
And the award always goes
to he who robs the most.

The Mayor and the Priest
of my home town
have taken possession of a farm
without doling out any cash
isn't that first-class!

Gaurkua da edade
Justiziarik ez dana
Negarrez dago zeru altuan
Ama Birjina laztana.

Onen gainian esan biar det
bertso oneitan egia
Nai asarratzen bada nirekin
justiziaren begia
Nola gogorregia
Da nirekin legia
Oiekin berriz suabia
Ala ni ere izango nintzan
Jaunaren bildur gabia.

Euskalerrian jaio ez banaiz
ikasi nuen dotrina
Ez da zilegi bidegabia
bilau farisiok ina
Negarra ta zotina
Da niretzat propina
Nik irabazitakua
Etor dakidan barkaziua
Jaunaren grazitakua.

Nekazaritzan aita guriak
ondasuna zuan galdu
Eta arduen merkataritzan
gero ederki ugaldu
Demoniuak baldu
Infernua bigaidu
Inor denpora sikuan
Ola birritan gure aitaren
onrak ondatu zituan.

Nire guraso biak ziraden
jaio Bizkaiko lurrian
Aragoiera azaldu ziran
gure Amaren aurrian
Zarakoza zarrian
Ez ain leku txarrian

This is an unjust age
where what passes as law
will make Our Lady in Heaven
cry and cry and cry.

Above all in these verses
I must tell the truth
even if the eye of the law
crinkles and loses the plot
and deals me harsh justice
while others a soft hand
oh well, never mind
that's what I'm like
godless, unafraid.

Although I wasn't born
in the Basque Country
I've learned the doctrine,
the crime of the Pharisees
is not what it seems.
Tears and hiccups
are my winnings,
my way to earn
God's forgiveness.

Our father lost a fortune
dealing with agriculture,
but earned another handsomely
when he swapped to wineries.
The devil never sends
his acolytes dry to hell,
and thus He twice destroyed
my father's honor and his name.

My parents were born
in the land of Bizkaia.
Then they moved to Aragon,
to live in old Zaragoza* town
across Our Lady,
which is not the worst

Euskalenitik Kanpuan
Ango jentia ez det egingo
laudatu nire kantuan.

Amasei urte nituanian
gerrara ziraten deitu
Karlosen kontra kiristinuak
soldau ninduten esleitu
    Proklama batzuk leitu
    Patu txarrak bete itu
Nik zer egin biar nuan
Onela eman nituan pauso
triste batzuk infernuan.

Ola ikusi nuan lenengoz
arbasuen sorterria
Fueroen kontra isuri nuan
nire odolan erdia
    Ni ez nintzan erbia
    Ni ez nintzan zerria
Ongi nintzaden portatu
Prisionero eroritare
nai ez ninduten urkatu.

Gerra bukatu nire etxera
aguru nintzan abitu
Bular onetan pozaren pozez
biotza ez zan kabitu
    Nik ez nuan aditu
    Gerrak atera ditu
Mila bidegabe ilun
Guraso bien azternik ere
ez nuan bilatu inon.

Lau urte luze dira gerrara
sakabanatu naizala
Ama Birjina Pilarrekuak
ongi anpara nazala
    Umezurtza bezala
    Kristau onen azala

but it's no Basque Country either.
For the people who live there
I really don't have the words.

I was only sixteen
when I was called to fight.
Christians made me a soldier
to fight King Carlos' wars.
        I was read this pamphlet
        my fate went down the toilet
there was nothing I could do
but walk my sad shoes
into this hell, this limbo.

That's how I first laid eyes
on my ancestors' homeland.
Half of my own blood
I spilled to fight the Old Laws
        I wasn't a hare
        I wasn't a pig.
I believed in what I did.
And although I was caught
they wouldn't hang me.

Once the war was over
I ran all the way home.
My heart didn't fit in my chest
such was the size of my happiness.
        I never knew the crimes
        war can bring to your door
for much as I looked and looked
my parents were nowhere to be found.

It's been four long years
since they banished me to war
and I beg for the protection
of Our Lady of Pilar
        save this Christian's skin
        keep this orphan from risk

Arriskuen ingurutik
Nire aitamak il dituztela
ez det kenduko burutik.

Nire aitaren etxe aurrian
Izan ez nuan atsegin
Modu zipriztin eta gaitzian
birauka nuan itzegin
        Ura gerta ez zedin
        Ala eta utsegin
Zezaten pentsamentuak
Bakarrik etxe ari geratzen
zitzaizkion zimentuak.

Zeruan daude bi martiriak
ez daukat zer egin aika
Edo barneko sentimentuak
eta min garratzak aipa
        Galdu nuala aita
        Gaxua izan baita
Oso debil eta flako
Eriotzia eman zieten
Bizkaitarrak ziralako.

Baina lenago portxatu zuten
amatzo biotzekua
Au da azio lotsagarria
edozein urkatzekua
        Afusilatzekua
        Ez nik barkatzekua
Gero ziguten lapurtu
Modu onetan zuten Jaunaren
lege santua apurtu.

Gizonak mundu onetan ber du
ongi pentsatu lenengo
Ola ainbeste zorakeria
desleial ez zan egingo
        Ala nola banengo
        Zoro nion emango

in my mind I know, I'm certain,
that my parents have been killed.

I have no worthy memories
from this visit to our home.
I said terrible things, shouted,
blasphemed and cursed the world
    how I wish it wasn't like this
    how I wish my mind had won
over the knowledge that my home,
the place where I was born,
was nothing now but bones.

The two martyrs are now in Heaven
so I've nothing to complain about,
no reason to say how I feel
or display the colors of my pain.
    Know that I lost my father,
    know that he was weak,
always thin and always sick.
The only reason they both died
is that they were born Basque.

But first they raped my mother,
love of my heart,
and the injury of this shame
is enough to kill and maim
    to hang, to shoot,
    to never forgive.
Then they stole it all
and like this they broke
God's sacred laws.

In this world man must know
to think before he acts
to avoid doing things
that are disloyal and mad.
    So crazy I was I said
    it was right and proper

Au zan nire arrazoia
Zarakozako alkatiari
Fusil baten kargazoia.

Au erostera nindualarik
topatu nuan birian
Euskalerriko aldiano bat
oso jator agirian
    Ni ez naiz inbirian
    Ok nola bizi dian
Ez beintzat paradisuan
Pozgarritxo bat aurkitu nuan
orduko pasadizuan.

Galdetu nion nungua zan da
aren erria Zornotza
Lurralde orrek ikusi zuan
nire aitamen jaiotza
    Pozik ene biotza
    Ez det zergatik lotsa
Senidiak ditudala
Mutil egoki ura zalako
nire gusu naturala.

Ezaguera zelebratzeko
topa genduan taberna
Nafarruako ardo gorria
Gipuzkuako lanperna
    Nun zeguen galerna
    Argitzeko linterna
Atera ginan ordirik
Trenbire ura gelditutzeko
ez zan bandera gorririk.

Nire lengusu maitagarria
ez zan ain mutil ergela
Zakarragua izan da beti
udazkenian orbela
    Nola zabiltz orrela
    Bilbotik zetorrela
Idi biak arriatzen

to shoot the Mayor of Zaragoza,
to kill and finish him myself
with a fully loaded musket.

And on my way to buy one
I met on the road
a Basque farmer,
very friendly, and very nice.
        I'm not jealous of such people,
        their lives are no paradise.
But I found comfort
in the encounter
and what followed afterward.

I asked where he came from
and he said from Zornotza.*
That very same soil
hosted my parents first home
        and my heart skipped
        I feel no shame in this
he was family
handsome and strong,
my first cousin I had found.

To celebrate our meeting
we hit upon a bar
where we ate barnacles
and drank rosé from Navarre.
        Where was the lamp
        to light up this storm?
We got drunk.
No red flag could get
this train to stop.

My loveable cousin
was no fool after all.
We look down on the leaves
that go down in the fall.
        Why are you here?
        I came from Bilbao
with two oxen pulling a cart

Zarakozara gurdi aretan
gatz zuria karriatzen.

Itaurreneko bire luzia
ez da bire egokia
Idi ezkerra geldia bada
bestia berriz lotia
    Nun ote da dotis
    Aurkitzeko tokia
Merkia da karriua
Modu onetan ez det pagako
alabaren arriua.

Gaurko kamio eta estartak
ez dira oso errezak
Gerra bukatu berria dago
guztiz dira aldrebesak
    Ok dira esamesak
    Ez pagatzeko mezak
Aita nirekin nenkarren
Gurdiak bulka egin zigun da
aita il zan Baratzarren.

Nire aitaren korputz santua
lurilan zeguanian
Berialaxen paratu nintzan
kargatutzeko lanian
    Gurdiaren gainian
    Oso modu onian
Begiak zerratutzeko
Eta gatzian kanpo santura
ongi kontserbatutzeko.

Bizkaian txarki bizitu gera
ez gaude Andaluzian
Amaika duro irabazteko
ofizio itsusian
    Oso bire luzian
    Espainia guzian
Daramat nire gurdia
Ortik atera detan dirua
izan da guztiz urria.

all the way to Zaragoza
carrying white salt.

Guiding oxen along a road
is no task for the meek.
If the left one is slow,
the other prone to yawn.
    Where in this world
    am I to find riches?
Pulling carts is cheap,
so if I do this you see
my daughter's trousseau is fixed.

Today's roads and highways
aren't easy to navigate.
War is just over
so they're in a terrible state.
    With all the squabbles and mess
    who has the money for mass?
I brought my father along
but the cart unfortunately flipped
and in Barazar* he passed.

My father's holy corpse
had just hit the ground
immediately I got around
and fixed the upturned mound.
    His body went on the cart
    and I covered it in salt.
I closed his beloved eyes
hoping to preserve him intact
all the way to the churchyard.

We were poor in Bizkaia,
Andalusia is not as hard.
To earn some coin
in this tough job
    I pull my cart down and up
    every road on every map.
And the money that I make
with all the sweat and every ache
is really not that great.

Txirrinkak txistu egiten zuten
pronto gelditu gurian
Edo bestela gogorrik laban
egiten zuten eurian
Kalonjiak urian
Debalde Biturian
Eman zion oliua
Olan alperrik ez zedin galdu
gatz onaren baliua.

Biok gurekin generamala
gurdi artan eriua
Konturatu zan jakin gaberik
zein zan erremediua
Bertako meriua
Jainkua mediua
Biar zuan enterratu
Euskalerrian egiten dira
zaldiak alan perratu.

Mutil gaztiok beraren kontra
egin genduan burruka
Gizon portitzak ginala inork
ezin zezakian uka
Gaiztoki zedin buka
Karraisi ta oiuka
Ebrora genduan bota
Aragoieko moldian jantzan
egin zitzan amar jota.

Beraz igesi genduan eta
atakatu Naparrua
Gutzaz mendeka ez zedin gero
gure merio arrua
Ni ez naiz txitxarrua
Dauzkana lau arrua
Bernak baditut azkarrak
Ni bezalaxen buru gogorrak
dirade beti astarrak.
Irureraño eldu baño len
euskaraz genduan entzun

The wheels whistled
as they come to a halt,
or they slipped suddenly
when they lost against the rain.
    In Bitoria* the canon
    anointed him for free
that way, he thought,
the good salt
would still be worth something.

As the two of us traveled
with his body in the cart
I don't know how exactly
we knew to do what we must.
    For our custom dictates
    that it's God's mandate
to bury a body within a day.
That's how wc shoe horses
in the Basque lands and in Biscay.

We were young and strong
and a policeman, though he tried,
couldn't get us to give up,
our plan would not be denied.
    We threw him in the river
    and he shouted, he screamed,
and in the Ebro he danced a jig,
ten times they turn in Aragon
in these *jotas* that twirl and twirl.

This is why we ran away
why we crossed over to Navarre,
to escape the proud policeman
and avoid his punishment.
    I'm not the runt of the litter
    skinny and late to bloom.
My legs are fast, built like trunks.
And the donkeys in the farmsteads
are just like me, headstrong.
Before we arrived in Pamplona-Iruñea
we heard Basque being spoken.

Nire lagunak aitaren alde
euskaraz otoitz egin zun
Nik erdaraz erantzun
Biok daukagun zentzun
Andi eta aproposa
Aurrerantzian ez da egingo
nire biotzian poza.

Aste askoren buruan ginan
baserrira allegatu
Euskal garbia ikasitzera
gogor nintzan enplegatu
Askotan ernegatu
Geienetan negatu
Ori da gauza nekeza
Eskola artan ikusi nuan
andia nire flakeza.

Errezo franko aditu zuan
aitaren korputz ustelak
Dirutan ongi kobratu zuan
ango parroko ezkelak
Opil eta pastelak
Txokolate mistelak
Ederra okasiua
Modu orretan irabazteko
Jaunaren barkaziua.

Berialaxen juan ginaden
erriko kanpo santura
Egun artako ordu garratzak
datozkidala kantura
Erori naiz kontura
Nun ote da mentura
Nora guaz azkenian
Pentsatzen nuan nire osaba
enterratu zutenian.

Itsas aldetik dator aizia
gureganantza iparra
Lañoz betetzen dirade baso

My companion prayed for his dad
in the tongue they both shared.
  I replied in Spanish
  for we both have good sense.
I knew that from there on
in my heart my joy, my peace
would be forever gone.

After many weeks passed
at the farmstead we arrived,
and there I undertook
to learn the purest Basque I could;
  often I'd grumble
  mostly I'd stumble
because it isn't an easy endeavor,
in undertaking it I learned
to separate can from can't.

His father's rotten corpse
received so many prayers
the town's cross-eyed priest
found his pockets bulging.
  There's never been such a wake
  so lush with chocolate and cake,
*mistela** sweet wine and cookies.
Isn't that the best of ways
to ask for Heaven's forgiveness?

Very soon we all headed
to the town cemetery
and how I recall the pain
of the bitterness I felt.
  How as I walked I realized
  the fate of my enterprise.
So this is the final rest . . .
that's what I heard myself say
as my uncle sunk into the soil.

Look how the northerly wind
blows toward us from the sea.
The valley, the high mountain,

altua eta ibarra
    Zertarako negarra
    Ta sufritu biarra
Ez gaitezen orain trista
Gizon guztiak iltzen gerala
eman dirate albistia.

Kanpo santura aldapa gora
ez zan ain gauza ederra
Giltzurrunari ematen zion
ez aguntatzeko gerra
    Bizkaitarraren berba
    Esaidazue zer da
Niria det empeñatu
Nik ez derala iñoiz egingo
inor ere engañatu.

Alan zin egin nuan beraren
korputz ilaren gainian
Eta ginera nire guraso
bien oroitzapenian
    Nire fede onian
    Eta maitasunian
Ez naiz inoren zorduna
Nire diruaz pagatuko det
jango deran babarruna.

Mundu ontara jaiotzak eni
ekarri ziran malurra
Eta gizondu nintzadenian
zoritxarraren gailurra
    Zerutikan elurra
    Ta oinetako lurra
Au zan nire ondasuna
Jangoiko portitz eta liberal
orrek eman didazuna.

Ez nintzan garai artan Bizkaiko
bizimoduen ezagun
Erdalerritik elduta gero
en nenguan euskaradun

its forests, covered in mist.
Why then cry,
why be sad?
Because now I know
because they told me:
this is it, we're always dying.

The upward climb to the cemetery
wasn't really all that lovely.
My kidneys didn't like it,
oh God the steepness of it.
Tell me what's the word
of a Bizkaian man like.
Mine I had to pawn,
I swore I would never
harm or deceive another.

This I promised before his corpse
and on the memory of my dead,
of my mom and my dad.
I did so in full knowledge
with all my faith,
with all my love.
I owe no one nothing
and beans and sausages I'll eat
because with my sweat I'll earn it.

Being born into this world
has really not brought me joy
and as I grow into a man
new peaks of sorrow I find.
Snow from the Heavens
and the soil under my feet
those are the only blessings
awarded to me by a God
who is generous and strong.

Back then I wasn't familiar
with the Bizkaian way of life.
Just arrived from Romance land,
I couldn't speak Basque.

Orain batere lagun
Ofendi ez dezagun
Egia esango degu
Jesukristoren pasiotikan
artu biar det eredu.

Kristau askoren fede gogorrak
ez du biar ezein auspo
Karidaderik ez daukatela
biotza da burdinazko
Zamari eta asto
Ortik dabiltza asko
Jainkuaren izenian
Kondenaruak izango dira
Zeruratzen naizenian.

Jesukristoren Lege Santua
ez da ain gauza gogorra
Eta kristauen borondatia
ez da birtute agorra
Geroko derrigorra
Il ezkero zigorra
Munduan amodiua
Osterantzian emango diot
nire azken adiua.

Eldu berria naguan erri
orrek ez dirudi dama
Beti prezio karu batian
gordetzen duana fama
Ori da nire ama
Ta berekin darama
Odolian luzemia
Ala ta guzti deklaratzen naiz
Euskalerriko semia.

Euskal bertsotan alegindutzen
naiz zorionaren bila
Euskal kristauen fede zintzua
ez dedin izan debila

So as not to offend
friends and acquaintances
I will tell only the truth
and take as my inspiration
the Lord Christ's passion.

The faith of some Christians
is tough, needs no bellows.
Their sense of charity amiss,
their hearts spit and hiss.
These days too many horses
prance around with asses
take the name of God for granted.
All of them will rot in hell
on the day of my ascent.

The Sacred Law of Jesus Christ
is not that hard a thing
and the will of all Christians
far from a fruitless whim.
The thereafter for sure
is death and what comes after
and in the end only love matters.
If it wasn't so
right now I'd say *adieu*.

This country that I've come to
isn't like a dame
that keeps high
the price of her fame.
She is my mother
and carries inside her
a cancerous kind of blood.
Despite that I anoint myself
her most beloved son.

I always try in my Basque verses
to speak about happinesses,
so the faith of Basque Christians
shows no cracks, no weaknesses.

Emen nago umila
Ta nire kontra mila
Erretore diru zale
Irtengo dira Satan diabru
infernutarraren alde.

Oneik dirade pentsamentuak
niri menditik errira
Arin etortzen zitzaizkidanak
nere arima erdira
Gogo oneik zer dira
Nere etxe berrira
Kontentuz natorrenian
Ez nintzan ala ni portatuko
trantzerik gogorrenian.

Itsas onduan mariatzeko
ez det ikusten batela
Nire diruaz beteko dute
lapur gaiztuak sakela
Au da nire papela
Jantziko det txapela
Apaiz jaunaren aurrian
Alkate ori urkatuko det
baratzeko intxaurrian.

Nola niria izan dan beti
oso portaera zurra
Mila zatitan ausizidaten
gero buruko azurra.
nik ez diot gezurra
Artuko det aitzurra
Au da nire zoritxarra
Nigatik orreik esaten dute
naizala gizon litxarra.

Itz laburretan kontatuko det
nire penen kontaera
Argi ta garbi esplikatzeko
gizon oien portaera

Here I am, humble and
against me a thousand
money-loving priests
who will come out in defense
of Satan the dark beast.

Such were the thoughts
that plagued my soul
as I climbed down the mountain
on my way to the town.
Why this gloom
as I'm walking home,
a place that fills me with joy.
I never believed
I'd turn into this boy.

I don't know what ship
will sail me these seas.
These evil thieves will pocket
any money I see.
And that's the part I play,
my beret I'll wear
to face the holy priest,
while the mayor I'll definitely hang
from the walnut that faces east.

Because my path always followed
what they call the straight and narrow,
they ground my skull
into a bag of gravel.
I'll never tell lies
I'll gaze at the skies.
Such is my damn luck,
they say it behind my back:
I am a vile man.

I'll use a few short words
to tell the story of my woes
to explain once and for all
why man does what he does.

Kontsolatzen bagera
Adanen edadera
Ez gara allegatuko
Eta Jaunaren bendiziuak
ez zaizkigu edatuko.

Zerua dago goibelik eta
lañua dabil ibaian
Alako egun asko ikusten
dirade sarri Bizkaian
Nekazariak laian
Duaz azken amaian
Pobreza andi batera
Jainkuak eman bezaie laster
mejoratzeko aukera.

Orain artian izan naiz beti
nire buruaren jabe
Orregatikan modu gaitzian
ala gorrotatzen nabe
Beti egun ta gabe
Ala esaten dabe
Naizala gizon gaiztua
Benkatutzeko sartuko duste
sabel erdian aiztua.

Bata bilaua guztiz da eta
ez ain prestua bestia
Bi oien kontra ez da irtengo
ezer espada nastia
Emango det tristia
Dubarikan astia
Ala fabore deiegun
Desiertuan pasatuko det
baraurik berrogei egun.

Orko ilunpe itsugarriak
benetan dira sarriak
Lurrian kontuz jarritzen ditut
nire begi atzarriak

Because if we just accept things
we won't live like Adam did
then we'll be missing
all the Lord's blessings,
and we won't learn a thing.

The sky has darkened
and mist cloaks the river,
this is the nature of days
very often in Biscay.
Chasing the land
farmers mostly find
that it all ends in poverty.
I hope God soon grants them
some greater opportunity.

I've always owned my mind
right up until this day
that's why so many hate me
in such a vicious way.
Night and day
all they say
is that I am the baddie.
I await the vengeful dagger
that pierces my belly.

Where one is the definite villain
and the other not quite that good,
let's face it not much can emerge
from the blending of the two.
How sad I am
to have wasted my time
so their lives can be a little bit better.
Forty days without food in the desert,
if that'll teach me – I will do it.

The blinding shadows down below
are very thick and scary.
My hungry eyes scan the floor
slow and carefully.

Ortik erruz arriak
Apropos ezarriak
Ikusten ditut berriro
Goiko ta beko lanbro andiak
urratu dira argiro.

Goiko zerutik gordetzen dira
lurbirako gobernuak
Bildurragatik egiten dira
ikaratu infernuak
Ala dio sermuak
Jangoiko eternuak
Zaintzen ditu artegiak
Bide okerrak argitzen dizkit
Neska baten aurpegiak.

Amodinaz lurrera dua
nire biotza gainezka
Gaurko goizian ezagutu det
maitatuko nauan neska
Badaukat nori eska
Arindutzeko kezka
Ariman barrenekuak
Maite orrekin izango ditut
egun zorionekuak.

Neskatxa polit eder galanta
zu zara nire gozua
Amodiuaz egun batian
artuko dizut mosua
Ala dabil zozua
Ez ain itxurosua
Piko elduak jan gura
Iluziuan zure portuan
bota biar det aingura.

Alegrantziaz beterik dago
ni bizi naizan auzua
Arantza dua abiaduraz
ematen deran pausua
Izango zara zusua

There are many rocks
placed there *a propos*
I see the mists bealow and above,
in the mountain, in the valley,
bursting toward light airily.

From high above in Heaven
earth's governance is kept.
Hell dwellers are afraid
of the great fear that's felt.
That's what sermons say,
that God the eternal father
keeps the flock out of harm's way.
All I can say is that a girl's face
illuminates my life's lost ways.

My heart rolls onto the soil
overwhelmed, full of love,
today by chance I met
she whom I adore.
Now with her I can share
my heart's every concern,
my pain, my disappointment,
and she'll console me, I know,
and we'll find contentment.

Beautiful, gorgeous, elegant girl,
you are everything I dreamed
and one day your lips I'll kiss
with all the love that is in me.
Like a disoriented thrush
drunk on overripe figs
I admit I may look a bit silly.
All the same I must lower my anchor
in your port and no other, my lovely.

There's nothing but pure joy
in my neighborhood today
and my feet danced a jig
all the way right here.
Because you're the dove . . .

B): Astepeko sekretarioaren bertso zaharrak

Hemen nago, pelota-tokian
hemen, plaza erdian.
Garraisiok entzunen dirade
edonundik herrian.

Hemen jaikitzen naiz
negarrez,
zerri ta zorri batzuren kontra
fugerte deiadarrez.

Eskubian ikusten dut
eliza,
eta ezkerrean herriko etxea
digante baten gisan.

Euskalerrian bakarra,
hegaz dabil zikoina.
Hemengo basatzan sartzen
zaiola kasik oina.

Herri honetan eztago
inor kontentu:
Agintariek eztute
batere fundamentu.

Egia garratzak kantatu nizkien
bertsotan;
horregatik eznaute hartuko
maitakiro besotan.

Nire etsaiak izan dirade
zorria eta zerria,
haiengandik kopetatik atera zait
oparo izerdia.

Gizonak izan dirade beti
gizonaren etsaiak.
Ardiak zergatik maitatuko ditu

B): Old Verses by Astepe's Secretary

Here I am in the pelota court
here where we play this sport
my shouts reach everywhere
from bell tower to cot.

Here I now stand upright,
distraught,
upset by the pigs and the lice,
screaming my lungs out.

On the right I see
the church
and the town hall to its left
standing gigantic, huge.

Only the stork flies
above Basque lands,
its feet almost stuck
in the mud baths.

No one is happy
in this here country,
everything politicians do
we just boo.

I spoke bitter truths
in my verses
that's why I don't expect
kind embraces.

My enemies have always been
the pig and the lice
it's because of them that I suffer
all that sweat above my eyes.

Men have always been
the enemies of men
why should the sheep

artzaiak?
Nola gorrotatzen dudan orain
Iparragirren boza;
ezin dezaket oraintxe
puntu gaitzikan goza.

Orain mintzatzen naiz
lehengo berso zaharrean;
nola esplikatuko naiz
nire euskera meharrean?

Muskerrak eta sugeak zaizkit
ahotikan atera;
honela ez naiz helduko
zeru goien batera.

Nire ahoak dirudi
Donibane Sanjoan;
eztakit zer etorriko zaigun
bizitzaren ondoan.

Iregi bitez ateak,
zabal bitez leihoak;
ikus dezaten guztiek nola
hiltzen garen lehoiak.

Etor bitez herriko guztiak
orain nire aurrera,
orain nire aurrera,
ikas dezaten nigandik nolakoak diren
infernuko sarrerak!

Azkenean sartu behar naute
kalabozoan.
Leku atseginean bizi garade,
hala, gozoan.
Nire bizitzaren kontaera
kontatu nahi nuen.
Iparragirren boz ederrean
kantatu nahi nuen.

love their shepherd then?
And now I totally hate
Iparragirre's voice,
I can't for the life of me tell,
what was it that I enjoyed?

Now I am singing
old style verses,
can my Basque ever contain
something of substance?

Out of my mouth
spill lizards and snakes,
it's unlikely that I'll reach
the southern heavenly gates.

My mouth reminds me
it's Saint John's day;
so what becomes of us
once we die?

Open wide all doors,
fling open all windows,
let everyone see
how death treats lions.

Have everyone in town now
stand before me
stand before me
let them learn from those who know
the gates of hell and their openings.

They'll throw me in the hole
in the end.
That's the paradise we live in,
that's what we call home.
The story of my life
I wanted to tell,
I wanted to yell
in Iparragirre's voice.

Baina jentea niri entzunik
aspertuko da;
nire gauza, nire hauzia honela, nola
aztertuko da?

Herri honetan kantatu
egiten da debalde,
inork ezpaitu irtenen
sekula nire alde.

Ni naiz bertsolari hain traketsa,
kantore txit torpea;
nirekin ezlitzake kontentatuko
Pariseko gortea.

Ni baino barregarriagorikan
ezta ezein pailazó;
hain trankil ezta biziko inor,
hain lazo.

Badakit zer iguriki didan
mundu honetan,
zergaitikan bizi naizen beti
penetan.

Bizitza ez, ezta gauza atsegina,
ezta gauza ederra.
Okerbideari diot
emango nire gerra.

Gauzak gertatu diren bezala,
zergatikan dira gertatu?
Zergaitik hain asturu gaitzik zitzaidan
niri suertatu?

Bideak edonundikan doaz
mendiaren barrena,
lehena ahaztu gaberik
dator ehungarrena.

But I fear my story
will bore you all.
How then will my case, my questions,
inform you all?

Here people sing
for free,
because no one's about to come out
to defend me.

My improvised verses
are so bad, so out of tune
I'd never make it
in a Parisian salon.

There is no funnier
clown than me,
no one is calmer, lazier,
or leads a better life.

I know what the world
will bring me tomorrow,
I know because I live
in permanent sorrow.

Life isn't –nope– a fine thing,
it's no beautiful thing.
I'll give the war against injustice
my everything.

Why do things happen
the way they do?
Why can't I have
some better luck?

The paths into the mountain
are multifold,
before we forget the first one
the hundredth one unfolds.

Probak eman nituen nik
bertsolaritzan,
nire bertsoak Euskal herriak
kontsola ditzan.

Etorri nintzen Aragoietik
gure lurrera,
okerbidearen
gaineko gailurrera.

Ni naiz
naizena,
eztiot inori aipatuko
nire izena.

Astepeko Sekretarioa jarri
zaida izengoitia,
eta Matxalen Errenteriako
izan zen neronen esposa maitea.

Zergatikan inor ezta aterako
nire deiera?
Zergatik gizon-andreen prestutasunak
izanen ditu hogei era?

Zergatik eztu berdin tratatuko
aberatsa eta pobrea?
Zergatikan premiatuko du berdin
etoia ta noblea?

Bai. Zer da hau?
Hemen ni plazan?
Eztira oraindik enteratu
zer naizan?

Nire andre bihotzeko maitagarri dotorea
bortxatu dute,
honela nire deseoa
altxatu dute.

I proved my mettle
as a verse improviser,
I wanted my song
to make all Basques better.

I came to our land
from Aragon,
here to the jewel
in injustice's crown.

I am
who I am
and my name . . .
I'll keep mum.

They've renamed me
Astepe's* secretary
and my lovely wife
was Matxalen from Errenteri.

Why shouldn't someone
answer my call?
Why should human kindness
have twenty faces or none at all?

Why aren't rich
and poor treated equally?
Why should the noble
and ignoble be rewarded identically?

Yes. What is this?
Why me here in the plaza?
Don't they know yet
what I am?

My lovely darling wife of my heart
was raped,
and for this
my desire roared.

Nire etxe politean sartu ziren
lapurrak,
nobleagoa da
gure zakurra.

Nire seme frailearen
ebatsi zidaten kaliza;
hartzaz hornitzen da orain
eliza.

Gizon prestuen liburu haundian
ezta nire izenik.
Orain eztakit nik
gizon naizenik.

Ezta hemen
bide zuzenik.
Ezta hemen
gizonik.

Gizonak etxean
bildurtzen dira.
Andreak kalean
okertzen dira.

Zorri bi hoien esanetara
makurtzen dira,
eta honelaxen ohorea eta ondasanuk
lapurtzen dira.

Niri gertatu zaidana gero,
gertatuko zaio askori.
Nire bihotz hain leialak
badiost hori.

Bertso berrietan esplikatutzeko
hau zen luzea,
gizonen belarrietan
ezta dultzea.

Thieves entered
my beautiful house,
our dog
supports a finer cause.

They stole my son the priest's
Holy chalice,
and now the local church
displays it without malice.

My name doesn't appear
in the big book of noble men.
Now I don't know
whether or not I am a man.

Here there are
no righteous ways.
Here there are
no men.

At home men
shrink.
In the streets women
lose track.

They bow to the orders
of those two lice,
and that's how honor
and goodness get burglarized.

What happened to me then
will happen to others,
that's what
my loyal heart ponders.

To explain this in new verses
would have been too long
and the ears of men
aren't really that strong.

Madarikatua izan bedi
gizonen kasta.
Mundu honetan ezin diteke
trankilidaderikan dasta.

Nik esan behar dudana
ezta hain atsegina,
hau da nire protesta luzea
nik hitzegina.

Jesukristorik gabetan ezta
Ebanjeliorikan.
Hura gabe elizek eztute
baliorikan.

Maitatzen dut Jesukristo
bihotzetikan.
Okerra eta zuzena dira
bi hots etikan.

Harek juzgatuko gaitu
guztiak gero;
zuhur izanen garade batzuk,
besteak ero.

Orain esaten dudana
ez har kontuan,
potorik ezpaitut egin behar
puntuan.

Bertsolariak gagode beti
negurriak loturik,
bederatziko batean eztiet hoieri
eginen saluturik.

Hoek dira nire kontrario aldrebesak
Maitatu behar ditut.
Haien bertuteak
aipatu behar ditut.

Damned be
the human race,
there is no way in this world
to enjoy the taste of peace.

The things that I must say
are really not that nice
this ongoing protestation
is what I do with my life.

Without Jesus
there is no gospel
without Him
churches are nothing.

I love Christ
from my heart.
The difference between right and wrong
is not insignificant.

He'll judge us all
in the end;
some of us will be good,
others will descend.

What I say now
don't take into account,
I don't want to lose points
when it matters the most.

We verse singers
are gagged by rhyme,
with this here nine-syllable line, right,
how can I just say hi?

These are my sharpest antagonists.
I must love them.
Their virtues,
I must count them.

Jainkoak hoien bekatu latzak,
nolatan juzkatuko ditu?
Satan deabruaren azioak,
noiatan puskatuko ditu?

Plaza honetan eztago
inor entzule.
Haien galdereri eznatzaie oraintxe egonen
ni erantzule.

Nola diot inori esplikatuko
frutuen parabola,
iharrik badago
Gernikako arbola?

Nola diot inori esplikatuko
testamentu zaharra?
Nola adoratuko dut
Moisesen laharra?

Baldin eta oraindik ezpadakigu nun dagoen
arbola malatoa?
Txit odol garbikoak baldin badira
negroa eta mulatoa?

Nola errespatatuko dugu
Tabor mendia,
ezpaldin bazaigu bihurtuko
fuberoen mendea?

Euskalduna fededuna,
baina goiko zerutik
eztu inork eskribitu.
Hau diot zutik.

Euskalerriak hau dio
ditxo zahar batean.
Honela bizi gara gu
bakean.

How will the Almighty judge
these people's sins?
How will he undo
the evil Satan's will?

No one is listening
in this square,
how do they expect me to come up
with an answer?

How can I explain
the parable of the fruit
when the tree of Gernika
is dry as a nut?

How can I explain
the old testament?
How can I pray to the burning bush
that guided Moses in the desert?

What if don't know where the Malato tree
ended up,
what if the blood of the black man
runs as thick as yours or mine?

How can we respect
Mount Tabor,
when we don't know
if we'll ever get back the Old Laws.

The Basques are a faithful lot
but it's foolish to pretend
a mandate came from Heaven.
I mean it like I say it.

These are the words
of an old Basque song
this is the peace
our proverbs build.

Hau da euskaldun zaharren
legea,
eta euskaldun berrion
fedea.

Hemendikan ateratzen dena
ezta zilegi;
lege barnean sartzeko ikusten dut
difizilegi.

Eta zertarako aipatu behar dut
bestela
nik
Gaztela?

Begira nola nagoen
itsurik.
Zerrieri berriz eztiet nik
emanen abisurik.

Niri egin didatenak barkaziorikan
eztu merezi.
Jainkoak hauk juzgatuko ditu
gogorrik bihar edo etzi.

Eztakit zer duten irabazi,
edo zer galdu;
penak eginen zaizkio infernuan
ugaldu.

Orduan portesta jarritzen ezpadut,
eztaukat jeniorik,
hoiek ezpaitute
lortuko premiorik.

Hemen nago gartzela barnean,
honera naute sartu,
zerri eta zorri hoien kontra
nintzelako ausartu.

These are the Old Laws
of the old Basques,
and this the faith
of the new Basques.

What comes out of here
is not legitimate,
for the law to justify it
is just too intricate.

And why on earth would I,
at all,
mention
Castile?

Look how blind
I am.
I'll never warn the pigs
again.

What they've done to me
cannot be pardoned, ever,
God will judge them harshly
tomorrow and forever.

I don't know what they earned
or what they lost,
all I know is that their sorrows
in Hell will get a boost.

So if I don't continue my protest
it's because I'm no genius,
well you know,
I'm not getting any prizes.

Here I am in jail,
they locked me inside
because I dared stand up
to the pigs and the lice.

Hemen pagatzen dut
nire errurik eza.
Ni naiz
traketsa.

Merezi dut
zihorra.
Ni naiz
idorra.

Hemen
Maiz
Hiltzen
naiz.

Haien
zai
diot
bai.

Eztut
indarrik,
gizontasunaren
hondarrik.

Here I pay
for my zero culpability.
That's what I call
stupidity.

I deserve
the penance
because
I'm a dunce.

Here
I
often
die.

Awaiting
I
say
aye.

I'm
powerless,
exit
manliness.

NOTES

Downhill (Maldan behera)

p. 29 *this holy oak*. A reference to the Tree of Gernika, the revered oak tree under which lawmakers used to meet in Gernika, Bizkaia to craft public policy. The tree became a symbol of the *fueros* or laws defending Basque decision-making authority within the Spanish Kingdom and the oak metaphor, likewise, remains a potent representation of Basque singularity; also eulogized by William Wordsworth in "The Oak of Guernica" (1810).

p. 57 *River nymphs and the golden comb*. The line about river nymphs and the golden comb is likely a reference to the mythological *lamiak* of Basque folklore, lion-haired aquatic sirens who attracted people by combing their long hair.

p. 95 *Gernika turning into tears*. A reference to the bombing of Gernika, see note above on Gernika.

Rock & Core (Harri eta herri)

p. 133 *Lemoa*. Town in Bizkaia nine miles east of Bilbao. Known for its quarry.

Otxarkoaga. A working-class neighborhood of Bilbao made up of low-cost housing created specifically in the 1960s to house poor immigrants that had come to the Bilbao in the 1950s in search of work and were living in shanty-like conditions on the outskirts of the city.

p. 135 *Deusto University*. A private Jesuit university founded in the Deusto neighborhood of Bilbao in 1886.

p. 137 *Zorrotza*. A neighborhood in Bilbao historically important for its port facilities close to the center of the city.

p. 139 *Otero*. Blas de Otero (1916–1979) was a Basque poet from Bilbao who wrote in Spanish and was one of the leading exponents of social poetry in Spain in the 1950s.

Blas. Another reference to Blas de Otero.

Mikel Lasa. A Basque poet and writer (b. 1938) from Getaria, Gipuzkoa, noted for his revitalizing influence on Basque-language poetry.

Amaia Lasa. A Basque poet and writer (b. 1948) from Getaria, Gipuzkoa, the sister of Mikel Lasa and a pioneering woman poet.

p. 143 *Laudio*. Town in Araba twelve miles south of Bilbao.

Zarautz. Coastal town in Gipuzkoa thirteen miles west of Donostia.

p. 151 *Mount Artxanda*. One of the emblematic mountains surrounding and delimiting Bilbao.

p. 153 *Berango*. Town in Bizkaia ten miles north of Bilbao.

p. 155 *Euskara*. The Basque language in Basque (also spelled *Euskera* and *Eskuara*).

Gernika. Historically important town in Bizkaia, twenty-two miles east of Bilbao, it contains the "oak of Gernika," the site of traditional Basque government. It was also famously bombed by the German Condor Legion in April, 1937 during the Spanish Civil War, under the direction of the fascist Francisco Franco, an event that was the subject of Picasso's famous painting *Guernica* (the Spanish spelling of the town).

p. 157 *Altube*. The writer, philologist, and musician Seber Altube (1879–1963). He was the author of the influential book *Erderismos* on the proper use of Basque grammar.

p. 159 *Joxepe Mikel*. A reference to Father Jose Miguel Barandiaran (1889-1991), the great Basque anthropologist and ethnologist who carried out major archeological research as well as collected Basque legends and folktales.

Ataun. A town in Gipuzkoa, birthplace of Barandiaran.

p. 161 *Indautxu Square*. One of the main squares in central Bilbao, in the affluent Indautxu neighborhood.

p. 163 *Axular*. Pedro Agerre, known by the penname "Axular" (1556–1644) and from Urdazubi, Nafarroa, was arguably the leading Basque-language writer prior to the modern age, and famed for his novel *Gero* (Later, 1643) in which he incorporated his own rudimentary form of standard Basque.

p. 165 *Mount Gorbea*. Mount Gorbeia ia an emblematic mountain, just under 5,000 feet high, on the border between Bizkaia and Araba. In reality, Axular died in Sara, Lapurdi.

p. 169 *Joxepe*. Probably a reference to Joxe Azurmendi, a friend of Aresti who was at that time living in Arantzazu.

p. 171 *Arantzazu*. A reference to the Arantzazu Basilica, a Franciscan sanctuary located in the Aizkorri mountain range in Oñati, Gipuzkoa.

p. 177 *Saint Mammes*. Saint (San) Mammes was a semi-legendary third-century child Christian martyr who was thrown to the lions by the Romans. San Mames is also a district in the Olabeaga neighborhood of Bilbao, famous for the location of the Athletic Bilbao soccer club stadium.

Agnes. Saint Agnes, a virgin-martyr and one of seven women, who along with the Blessed Virgin, are commemorated by name in the Canon of the Mass. According to tradition her breasts were severed. On February 5 her memorial day is still celebrated throughout the Basque Country with groups of singers going house by house.

p. 179 *Begoña*. A reference to the Basilica of Begoña in a neighborhood of the same name in Bilbao, and dedicated to the patron saint of Bizkaia, the Virgin of Begoña.

Mount Urbi. Most likely a reference toMount Urbia, where arantzazu is located.

Zortziko. Literally meaning "of eight." A well-known and representative type of Basque melody and rhythm pattern usually transcribed in 5/8.

p. 181 *Oñati*. A town in the province of Gipuzkoa. The Arantzazu Basilica belongs to the jurisdiction of this town.

p. 189 *Jorge Oteiza*. Internationally acclaimed Basque sculptor (1908–2003) who renounced sculpture and went on to write key theoretical texts on Basque culture in the 1960s arguing for a new Basque aesthetics based on decomposition or the disoccupation of space and rooted in prehistoric art, specifically in the many cromlechs or stone circles that are found in the Basque Country. Famous for his sculpture of fourteen apostles in the Arantzazu Basilica, for his *Void, Construction* on Concha Bay of Donostia-San Sebastián, and many more works as well as participation in Basque cultural life.

p. 191 *Iparragirre*. A reference to the famed Basque troubadour Jose Maria Iparragirre (1820–1881), who spent much of his life in exile and assumed the mantle of a national bard for many Basques.

p. 193. *Txakoli*. A young dry wine native to the Basque Country, more typically produced as white wine, but also available in red and rosé varieties.

p. 195 *The Old Laws*. A reference to the *fueros*, the historical laws demarcating Basque decision-making authority within the Spanish Kingdom.

p. 197 *Basurto*. A neighborhood of Bilbao and location of the main city-center hospital.

p. 199 *Improvised verse singers*. A reference to *bertsolariak*, Basque-language versifiers who improvise and sing poems using different melodies that give them the basic metric structure and the points of rhyme at the end of each musical phrase or sentence.

p. 201 *Udarregi*. Juan Jose Alkain, known as "Udarregi" (1829–1895), was a *bertsolari* or improvising verse singer from Usurbil, Gipuzkoa. Because he was an illiterate farmer, many of his verses went unrecorded.

Basarri. Inazio Eizmendi, known as "Basarri" (1913–1999), from Zarautz, Gipuzkoa, was one of the foremost *bertsolariak* of his day, winning the national championship twice. By profession he was a journalist and he also published several books.

p. 203 *Gabriel Zelaia*. Gabriel Zelaia (also Celaya; 1911–1991) was a Basque poet from Hernani, Gipuzkoa who wrote in Spanish and was one of the leading exponents of social poetry in Spain.

Agustin Ibarrola. Agustin Ibarrola (b. 1931) is a Bilbao-born painter and sculptor who was part of the constructivist school in the 1950s and whose work has been imbued with social commitment.

p. 205 *the Arenal*. The main promenade by the old quarter and river in central Bilbao.

p. 207 *Aita Donostia*. Under the penname Aita (Father) Donostia, Jose Gonzalo Zulaika (1886–1956), a Capuchin priest from Donostia, was an influential Basque musicologist and composer.

p. 215 *Donostia*. Also known as San Sebastián, the capital of the Basque province of Gipuzkoa.

p. 217 *Bertsolari Day*. A day dedicated to celebrating *bertsolaritza* that started in 1968 with a tribute to the *bertsolari* or versifier Manuel Olaizola, "Uztapide" (1909–1983), and continued thereafter as a celebration of *bertsolariak* in general.

p. 219 *Nerbion*. Today spelled Nerbioi (or Nervión in Spanish), a river that begins its course in the Basque province of Araba (Álava) and joins the River Ibaizabal just prior to entering Bilbao where it becomes the Nerbioi Estuary that flows out to the sea.

p. 223 *Mundaka*. A coastal town in Bizkaia twenty-four miles east of Bilbao.

Arrigorriaga. A town in Bizkaia seven miles south of Bilbao.

p. 225 *lifting rocks*. Reference to *harri-jasotze*, a popular rural sport in the Basque Country in which stones of various shapes and sizes must be lifted off the ground and onto the shoulder.

p. 227 *Gipuzkoa*. The Basque province neighboring Bizkaia, whose capital is Donostia.

p. 229 *Zaragoza*. The capital city of Aragon.

p. 235 *Zornotza*. A town in Bizkaia, also known as Amorebieta, fifteen miles east of Bilbao.

p. 237 *Barazar*. A small mountain in Bizkaia south of Bilbao and leading to the Arratia Valley.

p. 239 *Bitoria*. A reference to Vitoria-Gasteiz, the capital city of the province of Araba and the current capital of the Basque Autonomous Community.

p. 241 *Mistela*. An alcoholic drink produced by adding alcohol to non-fermented or partially fermented grape juice. The addition of alcohol stops the fermentation, producing a very sweet beverage.

p. 249 *Astepe*. Astepe is a neighborhood in Zornotza (also known as Amorebieta), Bizkaia.